FAIR TRIAL
and
FREE PRESS

Fourth in the second series of Rational Debate Seminars
sponsored by the American Enterprise Institute
held at
The George Washington University
Washington, D. C.

FAIR TRIAL
and
FREE PRESS

Paul C. Reardon
Clifton Daniel

RATIONAL DEBATE SEMINARS

American Enterprise Institute
for Public Policy Research
Washington, D. C.

Library of Congress Catalog Card Number 68-8730

FAIR TRIAL and FREE PRESS

Paul C. Reardon

Clifton Daniel

Published by

American Enterprise Institute
for Public Policy Research

The First Amendment to the Constitution guarantees freedom of the press; the Sixth Amendment assures everyone the right to a speedy and public trial before an impartial jury. These two cherished pledges are difficult to balance when interpreted on one hand by the American press, and on the other hand by the legal profession. The problem could not be resolved by the eminent spokesmen for each profession in the American Enterprise Institute's Rational Debate Seminar on Fair Trial and Free Press.

The debaters are eloquent, well-informed—and combative. For the lawyers, the prolocutor is Justice Paul C. Reardon of the Supreme Judicial Court of Massachusetts. He chaired the Advisory Committee on Fair Trial – Free Press of the American Bar Association Project on Minimum Standards for Criminal Justice. His committee's report limiting the release and publication of crime news was adopted by the Bar's House of Delegates in February, 1968.

The report met with massive resistance in the editorial world. Sharply focusing this opposition is E. Clifton Daniel, the Managing Editor of *The New York Times* and a distinguished newsman with wide experience as a correspondent in the United States and in Europe.

Reporter-Attorney Fred T. Graham probably

summed up the dominant conclusion of this eighth AEI Rational Debate in his *New York Times* story on the third and final session: ". . . the two professions are still at swords' points over trial news coverage."

Each debater appeared once before a seminar panel of experts at The George Washington University, then met face to face for rebuttals in the third and final session at the National Press Club before Metromedia's television cameras. Many of the verbal exchanges are caustic, indicating the depth of feeling on this public policy issue among the press and the legal profession.

Judge Reardon, in the opening session, sums up the restrictions on crime and trial coverage that were adopted by the House of Delegates. The proposed rules, he says, stem from "abuses perpetrated allegedly in the name of a free press which tend to deny the individual right to fair trial."

His committee's recommendations, made after nearly four years of research, place restrictions upon attorneys, law agencies such as police, and trial judges. And through the limited use of the judicial contempt power, restrictions are also placed upon anyone (including the press) who disseminates information for publication willfully designed to affect the outcome of the trial, or on anyone violating a judicial order made in an effort to ensure a fair trial.

Lawyers would be barred from releasing information or opinion that would interfere with a fair trial. They could not give out details of an accused person's prior criminal record, the existence or content of any confession, the refusal of the accused to make a statement, the performance of any examination or test, the identity or credibility of prospective witnesses, the possibility of a plea of guilty to the charge, or any opinion on the accused's guilt or innocence. Lawyers could be reprimanded, suspended, or, in extreme cases, disbarred for violating the revised canon or the rule of court.

Judge Reardon recommends similar internal regulations for law agencies including the police. If these agencies failed to act, the regulations would be imposed by rules of the court or by legislation.

Judges would not be permitted to make any statement that might interfere with the fair trial. Judges could close pre-trial hearings to the public (including the news media) on motion of the defendant on the grounds that evidence or agreement in the hearing might disclose matters inadmissible to the trial.

Justice Reardon says he thought for a long time that "with some statesmanship," it would be possible to establish press-bar guidelines to which all would agree. He tried for two years to get a joint declaration of policy. Unfortunately, the joint declaration was impossible.

Mr. Daniel emphatically explains why.

The *Times* editor accuses Justice Reardon and his colleagues of "using a sledgehammer to kill a gnat," the gnat being "a tiny fraction of criminal cases . . . [that] . . . is ever reported in the press. And in only a fraction of this fraction is there any question of doing violence to the rights of defendants," Mr. Daniel adds. This heavy-handedness, he charged, "may wreck freedom of the press as well; it may shatter the very keystone of our democracy."

Mr. Daniel believes newspapermen have more faith in juries than lawyers have. "The juror who reads incriminating information about a defendant in his morning newspaper is just as likely to disbelieve the newspaper as he is to disbelieve the defendant—perhaps more likely," he says. "Nowadays, there seems to be a notion that the ideal juror is an intellectual eunuch, totally uninformed and blandly indifferent to his environment."

He agrees with Judge Reardon's idea for inservice training for crime news reporters. Mr. Daniel also favors voluntary press and bar fair trial codes, but he emphasizes the "voluntary."

"I have to say that I deeply resent, and so do my colleagues, the repeated implication by spokesmen of the legal profession that journalism is a shoddy, money-grubbing business with no morals, no scruples, and no ethics. We newspapermen do not believe that a law degree necessarily makes a man more honorable than a degree in journalism, or that elevation to the bench amounts to canonization."

"We must, in all conscience, resist those parts of the Reardon report that would make legitimate news unavailable to the public, make trials more secret, and allow judges to dictate what the press might publish," he declares. "We believe that the presumptuous attempt of the American Bar to prescribe rules of conduct not only for itself but also for the police and the press is unwise, unhelpful, unlikely to be effective, and is, in all probability, unconstitutional."

In rebuttal, Judge Reardon contends the bar standards do not "inhibit in any way the ability of the news media to write what they will about crime, court administration, corruption and public affairs, or any matter developed by the media through their own investigation or initiative." Rather than make things easier for the criminal defender, Judge Reardon argues his recommendations are trying to lessen the possibility of reversals of convictions of a "goodly number of crooks who ramble about our society on the grounds that their causes were prejudiced by publicity about them."

FOREWORD

This Rational Debate on "Fair Trial and Free Press" was the finale in the American Enterprise Institute's second series of four. It was also the first to be televised nationally. We are gratified to know that the Rational Debate format has shown itself to be adaptable to the broadcasting media, with their vast potential for reaching interested individual citizens with analyses of major public policy issues.

We are proud to add the names of Justice Reardon and Mr. Daniel to the list of distinguished participants in our Rational Debate Series. Earlier in the past academic year AEI sponsored programs featuring former Senator Paul H. Douglas and British Conservative Member of Parliament J. Enoch Powell debating "How Big Should Government Be?"; Yale University Professor James Tobin and Rochester University President W. Allen Wallis on "Welfare Programs: An Economic Appraisal"; and University of Chicago Professor R. H. Coase and Columbia University Dean of Journalism Edward W. Barrett on "Educational TV: Who Should Pay?"

June 25, 1968 William J. Baroody
       President
       American Enterprise Institute
       for Public Policy Research

PREFACE

Mr. Daniel and Justice Reardon, in this volume, bring us one of the sharpest confrontations in our Rational Debate series. Their learned analyses of the delicate balances between the fair trial and free press guarantees of our Constitution have become especially timely after the tragic assassinations of 1968 and the trials which lie before us as these words are written. Not only members of the bar and of the press, but interested readers of newspapers, listeners to radio, viewers of television and followers of the trials can find in these pages the means to judge for themselves how the news media and the courtrooms are safeguarding the constitutional rights of all our citizens.

June 24, 1968   G. Warren Nutter
                                      Coordinator
                                      Rational Debate Series

CONTENTS

FIRST LECTURE

PAUL C. REARDON

In a day when the country is mightily concerned with war, politics, and international finance, it might be argued that too much devotion to debate on the subject of fair trial and free press is unwarranted. However, this is an issue which antedates by many years all of those which have transcended it in recent importance, an issue which will remain unless it is resolved after some of the more immediate and pressing dilemmas have received appropriate solutions.

I propose to address myself to the problem, to the study of it which was made over many months by a committee of which I was chairman, to the recommendations which our committee made and which were adopted at the Mid-Winter Meeting of the American Bar Association in Chicago, to the reaction which the Chicago adoption generated, and finally to certain conclusions.

THE PROBLEM

First of all it should be emphasized that no American lawyer worthy of the name should ever forget the long,

hard-fought controversies which resulted in the First
Amendment to the Bill of Rights. Certainly the constitutional draftsmen, state and federal, most of whom
were lawyers, were well aware of them. They knew of
the proceedings in the Star Chamber and that it had
taken until 1641 to abolish it. They were familiar with
the case of John Lilburne who had in his trial before the
chamber upheld the rights of a free press and against
self-incrimination. They were familiar with the more
recent colonial history and the intolerance toward the
press of certain of the royal governors which produced
troubles in Virginia, in Massachusetts, and most notably
in New York. Our modern news media have many
times referred to the trial of Peter Zenger in 1734 and
1735 as a landmark and as a forerunner of what would
become at the hands of the constitutional draftsmen a
basic right in our democracy. Not to be forgotten relative to the Zenger trial was the part played by James
Alexander and Andrew Hamilton, Zenger's lawyers,
who staked their reputations and career upon his defense.
In my own state, John Adams, the principal author of
our Constitution of 1780, today the oldest working constitution in the world, placed before the Constitutional
Convention the Article which guaranteed to the press in
Massachusetts the now classic freedoms. This was 11
years before the adoption of the first ten amendments
to the federal Constitution. Since there has been talk in
recent days about "muzzling of the press" by judges and
lawyers, it is well for all to remember this early history,

to which I refer only briefly, and to recall also that part
of the heritage of the American bar is the defense of
freedom of the press. Time does not permit citation of
a host of instances in which the bar has undertaken that
defense. I can assure you that were attack designed to
stifle the free press of the United States leveled today
there would be no difficulty in finding counsel to defend
it. Lawyers have been at hand for this task over all the
years of the Republic and for many years before. Thus,
discussions on problems relating to the accommodation
of the rights of the press set forth in the First Amendment and the Sixth Amendment right of persons accused of crime to a speedy and public trial by an
impartial jury do not spring from an interest of the
American bench and bar contrary to the maintenance
of a free press. What we discuss here stems from abuses
perpetrated allegedly in the name of a free press which
tend to deny the individual right to fair trial. These
abuses in most instances do not originate with the press
at all, which is but doing its job in utilizing the information which comes to its attention.

Secondly, and prefatory to an indication of what has
bothered those who have studied press-bar problems, it
must be said that any solutions should be so defined that
the invaluable function of the press in routing out public corruption is in no sense hampered. One thinks back
to the newspaper work which brought Boss Tweed to
task in the early seventies or, more recently, activities by
the press which hammered at the Ku Klux Klan with

salutary results in the twenties. Reference is easy to any number of press campaigns which have resulted in great public good. News coverage undoubtedly expedited the apprehension of Richard Speck. No one can cavil at the "most wanted" lists of the FBI and the aid which press-published lists afford in picking up the eminent gentlemen whose names and faces are made prominent thereby. Furthermore, occasional abuses in criminal process deserve thorough airing. Brutality which sometimes occurs in enforcement agencies, failure to follow normal and required procedures in the case of derelicts, and a host of other troublesome situations often are most effectively relieved by press treatment. Informed and intelligent trial reporting is the best means of educating the public on the administration of criminal justice and perhaps the most solid guarantee that the trial participants adhere to the standards that our system of justice demands. Constructive criticism following a trial can serve to improve that system. Instances have occurred where discontent with the outcome of a trial has led individual reporters to investigate and to turn up evidence establishing the innocence of one wrongfully convicted. The value of these contributions in human terms cannot be overstated and no move to inhibit the press in its freedom to make these contributions should ever be made.

However, what has concerned thoughtful legal and press observers has been the other side of the coin. The problem came into dramatically clear focus in the events which occurred following the presidential assassination in 1963. The Warren Commission which studied them concluded that "the experience in Dallas during November 22 to 24 is a dramatic affirmation of the need for steps to bring about a proper balance between the right of the public to be kept informed and the right of the individual to a fair and impartial trial." As I have had occasion to state elsewhere, my own recognition of the existence of a situation which needed rectifying came in service as chief justice for over seven years of the jury trial courts of Massachusetts, as well indeed as meeting and talking in those years with dozens of trial judges around the United States. The American trial courts have lately been confronted with many perplexing questions. How does one resolve congestive docket delay in civil cases? What are fair sentencing standards? What is the most effective use of probation? What is the best method of judicial selection? And what should the tenure of judges be? All of these and others have served to test the ingenuity and the inventiveness of the judges who man our courts and all who are interested in them. The judicial contacts which I made, however, convinced me that no problem bothers the American trial judge more than that of how to ensure a defendant the trial to which our basic law entitles him.

It is not a puzzle of recent contrivance. It was once said, "Ours is the greatest newspaper reading population in the world; not a man among us fit to serve as a juror who does not read the newspaper. Every great and startling fact paraded in their columns, with all the minuteness of detail that an eager competitor for such favor can supply. Hence the usual question which has now become almost a necessary form in impaneling a jury, 'Have you formed or expressed an opinion?' is virtually equivalent to the inquiry, 'Do you read the newspapers?' In the case of a particularly audacious crime that has been widely discussed, it is utterly impossible that any man of common intelligence and not wholly secluded from society could be found who had not formed an opinion." The author who wrote this wrote it in 1846, 122 years ago. Ever since that time lawyers, judges, reporters, and editors have endeavored to resolve the dilemma described in that quotation. It has been asserted that the problem is limited in size, that most criminal indictments are disposed of by plea, and that we are concerned with a relatively small percentage of jury trial cases. The argument is made that the Brink's case, the Hauptmann case, the Sheppard case, and others of equal note are but a handful, and that what has been called "a pitiful little string of decisions" involving fair trial and free press should not become a very small tail wagging a very large dog. There have been a number of very informative books written in these last several years including one by Alfred Friendly and Ronald Goldfarb, and another by John Lofton. These gentlemen of the press have recited a list of cases tinged with prejudicial publicity from around the United States and described what occurred. The two volumes are replete with striking examples of the clash between rights of the press and rights of the defendant. To be sure, they deal largely with cases of local or national notoriety. It may be averred that as notorious cases they were an infinitesimal fraction of all the criminal matters heard or disposed of throughout the land in the years in which these examples took place. Yet it appears that from January, 1963, to March, 1965, a period of a little over two years, there were approximately 100 reported decisions in which the question of prejudicial publicity was raised. These reported decisions represent only the top of the iceberg, for heretofore the trial judge has been clothed with so much discretion in the area that it is fair to assume that the unseen portion of the iceberg comprised a very great number of matters indeed which never reached the appellate courts at all. In my view this reliance upon trial court discretion, already substantiated by some appellate language, is about to undergo change as evidenced some weeks ago by a unanimous decision in the Supreme Court of California critical of the manner in which the trial judge exercised his discretion. It is not to be forgotten that judges too may be affected by sufficiently pervasive publicity adverse to a defendant.

I also deem it a mistake to attempt to minimize the danger to the entire system of criminal justice generated by abuses in the notorious case, that is to say, the occasional case. As was stated by a witness several years ago before a Senate subcommittee, "It is only those cases which are already of a nature calculated to test most severely the fairness of the judicial process that arouse the interest of the press. These cases are numerically small but mirror the best and the worst of our vaunted claim to being a government under law. They are important exactly because they test the very fabric of our judicial system by placing the most stress upon it."

I have had occasion to review in the last three or four years a great many purportedly prejudicial news releases. I shall not belabor you with a recitation of a large number of these but here are some samples, with the names of the suspects in blank.

"John Doe, aged 44, charged with setting a fire that took the lives of a North Philadelphia mother and four children, was held without bail for a hearing October 8. Captain Joseph Rodden, head of the homicide squad, said that Doe when asked why he did it, replied, 'I don't know, I just went crazy.' "

Here is another. "San José police announced Saturday the solution of the purse-snatch murder of a retired nurse. Said Chief of Detectives, Barton L. Collins, of the twenty-one year old suspect, 'He is now definitely the man.' " This last sentence appeared in bold-faced type and there followed a detailed reconstruction of the crime by police.

I cite these examples, not particularly noteworthy except that they are examples, to indicate what is troubling those who are troubled in the area of free press and fair trial. The first example states the fact of the confession from the head of a prosecuting agency and assigns the reason of no reason for the crime. The second announces the solution of a murder, states who "definitely" committed it, and reconstructs the crime. Can it be argued that this type of reporting is not a dangerous assault on the right of the accused to a fair trial?

The hazards to fair trial have generally focused on the effect on a potential or actual juror. This effect is of course vital but it is not the only problem connected with publicity. To be considered also is the possible adverse impact of news coverage on the investigation of the crime, on the conduct of lawyers and judges, and perhaps most of all on the integrity of the judicial process and the stature of our legal institutions.

Relative to investigation, one thinks of the disturbance created by reporters in the efforts of police to recover the gems stolen from the Museum of Natural History in 1964. I have indicated that the press can be very helpful in investigation but a very rough indication of the reverse related to the kidnapping of a child in New York in 1956. There was a request for secrecy but one New York newspaper published the story, together with the kidnapper's instructions to the parents. The ransom money was not picked up; the child was abandoned in the woods and died of exposure. *The New York Times* then editorialized, "It is the business of a newspaper to report the news. Sometimes, however, a newspaper finds it necessary, or at least the humane thing to do, to stop and ask whether a given story should be reported, and when and whether a life may be put in jeopardy by premature publication of all or certain details. We regret that one New York newspaper apparently failed to do so."

Of course, the focal point of discussion in recent years has been the effect of publicity, which it may have read concerning the accused, on the jury which is ultimately chosen to try him. Empirical data which might tell us what that effect is is not at hand. Lord Coke declared over three centuries ago that the juror should "stand indifferent as he stands unsworne." This is not to say that a juror should have an ignorant or vacant mind. But it is important that each juror approach his task with no predispositions for or against a defendant which have come to him from what he may have read. It must be said that empirical data on juror prejudice, while desirable, would be extremely difficult to assemble. Jurors sometimes, as we have discovered, are not truthful on matters of possible prejudice. Frequently an individual cannot ascribe a cause for his action. The effects on the subconscious of a saturation of publicity are most difficult to sort out. It is difficult also to state whether every juror who says that publicity has given him a fixed opinion on guilt really entertains that fixed opinion or simply seeks relief from jury service. This much is true: there is a great deal in the reported cases indicating expressions by jurors who stated they held fixed opinions on guilt which could only have come from what they read. In the noted case of *Irvin* v. *Dowd,* out of 430 prospective jurors examined 268 were excused for cause as having fixed opinions of guilt, 90 percent of those examined admitted some opinion as to guilt, and eight of the 12 jurors finally selected admitted that they thought the defendant guilty, some saying it would take evidence to overcome their belief. In the notorious Brink's case, of 1,104 prospective jurors examined on the point, 659 admitted to having formed an opinion on the merits. There are reported instances of jurors consciously disregarding instructions given by the court in certain cases where they admitted seeing or hearing news stories about the case they were considering during the trial, although they were warned to avoid all such stories. In these instances admissions by jurors of what they actually read or heard are not easily obtained.

This and much more that could be said framed the problem of protecting fair trial. We proceed now to consideration of what in the last three or four years has been done about it.

THE STUDY

In 1964, three foundations financed a massive series of studies on the administration of criminal justice under the leadership of Chief Judge J. Edward Lumbard of the Second Circuit Court of Appeals. The Committee on Fair Trial-Free Press which I was asked to lead was added to the original group of studies dealing with sentencing, pre-trial procedures, and other aspects of the

criminal process as a result of a burgeoning sentiment in
that year that at long last the conundrum of how to
effect an accommodation between the First and Sixth
Amendments might be solved. Mine was a strong committee, comprising as it did federal and state judges,
teachers of the law, and men of extensive and varied
experience in the prosecution and defense of criminal
cases. We came together at the end of 1964 and proceeded to the first of a great number of meetings, many
of which were with representatives of the news media.
At our first meeting with them here in Washington
there was general agreement by all present that the problem did in fact exist. It appeared logical to move to
isolate it and endeavor to solve it. Certainly our committee, with that objective in mind, endeavored to remain
during the many months of our deliberations as open-
minded as possible. We assembled under the leadership
of our reporter, Professor David L. Shapiro of the
Harvard Law School, a research team. We initiated in-
quiries among judges and prosecution and defense counsel throughout the United States, with particular reference to metropolitan areas. I doubt that there is any
case in the area of Fair Trial-Free Press anywhere in the
English language that was not reviewed. We subscribed
to a selected but sizable group of newspapers over
lengthy periods of time. We sent investigators into certain American cities, one a single newspaper town where
the paper subscribed to a press-bar code; another a city
in New Jersey where *State* v. *Van Duyne* had laid down

certain guidelines; and another, San Francisco, a large city with newspapers in competition, where there were no recognized guidelines. We talked with leading police officials and law professors, and kept in touch with state and local bar associations engaged in tackling the Fair Trial-Free Press puzzle at local levels. We met with many judges, both federal and state. The series of meetings with representatives of the publishers, editors, and television and radio industries produced much suggestion which was helpful to us. We sent a research team to England and carried out studies there. Since we were charged to make recommendations relative to Canon 20 of the Canons of Legal Ethics, a canon which had never so far as the reports would indicate been enforced, it is entirely appropriate that I read it to you in the form which goes back many years: "Newspaper publications by a lawyer as to pending or anticipated litigation may interfere with a fair trial in the courts and otherwise prejudice the due administration of justice. Generally they are to be condemned. If the extreme circumstances of a particular case justify a statement to the public, it is unprofessional to make it anonymously. An *ex parte* reference to the facts should not go beyond quotations from the records and papers on file in the court; but even in extreme cases it is better to avoid any *ex parte* statement." The canon was demonstrably weak, inexact, and did not lend itself to enforcement. The recommendations which came at the end of our studies and which were adopted recently in Chicago are most importantly directed to a revision of that canon.

Prior to considering the recommendations, I wish to comment on our relationships with the media during the many months of study. The discussions which we had with them, which we carried on in a number of cities, were held on the friendliest of terms and in the spirit which had been in the mind of the Warren Commission when it urged study. It was my belief over a long period of time that with some statesmanship among all parties it would be possible to establish guidelines to which all would agree, and I bent every effort for over two years to the end that a joint declaration of policy might be made. Our study demonstrated that the points of difference between the media and the bar are comparatively few, but it was unfortunately impossible to come together on such a joint statement. This fact became extremely clear when on October 2, 1966, we released our recommendations.

THE RECOMMENDATIONS

The results of our work were contained in a report which with accompanying commentary and the results of certain studies comprised 265 pages, but the standards themselves are comparatively brief. They were directed to lawyers and to law enforcement agencies primarily. I shall review them with you.

Relative to lawyers, and it is in this field that we have recommended a revision of Canon 20, we stated that it is the duty of the lawyer not to release information or opinion if there is a reasonable likelihood that such dissemination "will interfere with the fair trial or otherwise prejudice the due administration of justice." We asked the lawyers to refrain with respect to grand jury or other pending investigations from making any extrajudicial statement that goes beyond the public record or that is not necessary to indicate the fact of an investigation or to obtain assistance in the apprehension of a suspect. We asked that from the time of arrest, the issuance of a warrant, or the filing of a complaint or information or indictment, until the commencement of trial or disposition without trial, a lawyer, whether he be with the prosecution or defense, not release details on the accused's prior criminal record, the existence or content of any confession, the refusal of the accused to make a statement, the performance of any examination or tests, the identity or credibility of prospective witnesses, the possibility of a plea of guilty to the charge, or any opinion on the accused's guilt or innocence. The foregoing is the nub of the revised canon. We have recognized, however, that the lawyer is free to announce an arrest and certain circumstances surrounding the arrest, to describe certain physical evidence other than the confession, admission or statement, which is limited to a description of the evidence seized and the nature of the charge, and is free also to comment on certain other factors. We have suggested that all of this be wrapped up in a rule of court, as well as adopted, as it will be now in the revised canons as the result of the action in Chicago. We further recommended that violations of the standards which I have described in broad terms should be grounds for reprimand, suspension, or, in extreme cases, for disbarment. All of this constituted Part I of the recommendations.

Part II recommended the adoption in each jurisdiction by law agencies of internal regulations paralleling those which we recommended for lawyers. We were of the opinion that where this was not done within a reasonable time that the standards for law enforcement agencies should be made effective by rules of court or by legislative action. As the result of certain information reaching us we also recommended the imposition on judges of the duty to refrain from any conduct or the making of any statement with respect to a pending criminal case that might tend to interfere with a fair trial.

Additionally, we recommended in Part III that with respect to pre-trial hearings the defendant might move that all or part of the hearings be held in chambers or otherwise closed to the public, including the news media, on the ground that evidence or agreement adduced at the hearing might disclose matters inadmissible at the trial. We left the closure of such hearings within the discretion of the trial judge, with the provision that a complete record of the preliminary trial hearing should be kept and made public after the trial or disposition of the case without trial.

Certain other recommendations in Part III dealing with court procedures which I shall not describe in detail followed in general the suggestions contained in the Sheppard case, although it is fair to state that they had been roughed out in committee discussions prior to the time that that case came down. These had to do with change of venue or continuance, standards for granting motions relative thereto, standards of acceptability of jurors, and conduct of the trial, including use of the courtroom, sequestration of the jury, and the cautioning of witnesses, parties and jurors. With these recommendations there has been little debate and I judge that they are generally acceptable.

Finally we urged a limited use of the contempt power against a person who disseminates for publication an extra-judicial statement relating to the defendant or the issues in the case that is willfully designed to affect the outcome of the trial and that seriously threatens to have such an effect; or against a person who knowingly violates a judicial order not to disseminate until completion of the trial specified information referred to in a hearing closed to the public. I emphasize that this is a very narrow application indeed of the inherent power of contempt which normally resides in the courts. I emphasize too that without it the courts would in effect be powerless to afford an accused the fair trial which he is entitled to receive. The provisions for contempt which really are peripheral to the main thrust of our report have created great consternation among the media. I suggest a careful reading of these provisions should offend no one.

These are the recommendations. It is important that they be understood for what they are. It is equally important that they be understood for what they are not. In view of the barrage of adverse editorial comment to which I shall refer presently, which followed upon the promulgation first, and the adoption second, of the recommendations, I should like to tell you what they are not and what they don't do.

1. They place no restriction on the news media to inhibit publication of essential information about crime and criminal investigations or the administration of the courts.

2. They do not restrict in any sense full coverage of trials or close any court records. While prior criminal records of the accused would not be officially released by prosecutors or law enforcement agencies, the news media could, if they chose to, publish what their own files contained.

3. They do not impinge in any way on the freedom of the press to expose corruption in the administration of public affairs or to criticize the courts on law enforcement.

4. They do not extend the contempt power of the courts but, on the contrary, narrowly define the areas in which that power is to be employed.

5. They do not seek to supplant voluntary codes of fair practice in crime news coverage developed by press-

bar groups in a number of states but rather serve to complement such codes by clear definition of the types of potentially prejudicial information which should not be released between arrest and trial.

6. They are not to be interpreted as providing a cloak of secrecy for lawyers and law enforcement officials relative to information about arrests and other steps in the judicial process which should be made public.

7. They do not restrict in any sense the exercise by the press in its investigative or "watch dog" roles of its freedom to publish findings developed through its own initiative.

I have referred to the meetings that we had with representatives of national organizations of the news media. It is possible now to designate at least 14 changes that were made in our recommendations arising from suggestions made at these conferences. We had, for instance, originally provided that in case of a mistrial stemming from an extra-judicial statement held to be in contempt of court that the court might require all or part of the proceeds of any fine to be employed to reimburse the defendant for additional legal fees or other expenses fairly attributable to the order that the case be tried in a different venue or tried again in the same venue. We excised this recommendation in the interest of coming as close as possible to the position on this point which the media representatives held. It is possible to cite other similar examples. We made changes where the media suggestions seemed sound and because we strove mightily to approach the point of view of the American press as closely as possible. It is to be emphasized that we did this freely and subject to no pressures whatever.

THE REACTION

When our recommendations were first released in October, 1966, there was a massive and generally adverse press reaction. With the exception of certain perceptive analyses made by a limited number of newspapers in their editorial columns, it was apparent to us that most of the comment came from writers who (1) did not understand the recommendations, or (2) chose to blanket them with general condemnation if they did understand them. Upon adoption of our work in Chicago in February, 1968, a similar reaction took place except that it seemed to me to be more shrill and unreasoning than the reaction of 16 months before. The privileges of the floor in the debate which occurred before the 289 delegates from the 50 states at the American Bar Association meeting were extended to representatives of the press who spoke forcefully and well and who sought delay in adoption on the basis of a study which was proposed to be made with the American trial judges. The motion for delay, which was made by a member of the House, was voted down 176-68. Thereafter a motion to adopt was carried on a voice vote. I have in these last weeks had the opportunity to review well over a thousand press clips on the Chicago action, as indeed I have reviewed since October, 1966, many thousands more of clips following the original release of the recommendations. I have read innumerable times that these recommendations were adopted on a shouted voice vote. We have been accused of formulating Star Chamber procedures. The association has been accused of taking precipitate action, as indeed it has been accused of hasty adoption which was the product of a motion. It has been said that the American bar favors secret trials, that the action in Chicago was one of arrogance, and that the association represents but one-third of the American lawyers in any event. To these charges one can only reply as follows.

The American Bar Association comprises 129,000 members. Of approximately 300,000 certificated lawyers in the United States somewhat in excess of 200,000 are in active practice, when one excludes those who are house counsel, in government service, retired, teaching, in business, or otherwise not actively practicing in the true sense. I hold no brief for the Bar Association except to state my belief that when the Bar Association speaks it speaks the voice of the American lawyer without question.

The names of the delegates from the 50 states were known to the press, and I venture the opinion that there was not one of them that was not extensively pressed prior to the Chicago meeting with reasons why our report should not be adopted. Our committee took no such action. We came to the House of Delegates on our proposals alone and endeavored prior thereto to sell the report to no one. The action of the House could hardly be deemed precipitate when our report had been out in the open for well over a year, had been thoroughly debated, including debates engaged in by representatives of the press at the Honolulu meeting of the American Bar Association last August.

I see no reason whatever to state that the report will result in secret trials. That certain evidence on pre-trial hearings is held for release until all danger of prejudice is over certainly is far removed from the classic attributes of the "Star Chamber" which so many of the press have belabored in recent weeks. Far from being arrogant, we sought information and help from every available source and weighed with care everything that came our way. We make no apology for our product and I am only saddened by some of the language which has been employed against us, not for ourselves and our recommendations but for the press itself which I am satisfied on this issue has little public support. I said over a year ago, and I repeat my view, that, in the discussions which have preceded today, the press has damaged itself rather than otherwise when a real opportunity lay before it to settle this issue once and for all by a rational and thoughtful approach to settlement in cooperation with the American bench and bar.

CONCLUSION

I should like to conclude with certain observations born of nearly four years of study and consultation. One could not come away from such an effort without holding certain views. I desire to express mine for what they are worth.

In the first place, the problem which we surveyed is just not going to vanish now that there has been a lot of talk about it. Our work should be continued by others. We have evidences of what we consider gross abuses in the reporting of crime which have occurred since the debate at Chicago. If there is to be a new level in the handling of crime news it seems clear that much remains to be done. It is heartening to note what has been accomplished. I agree with many of the media which asserted prior to the Chicago meeting in February that the impact of our committee has already been a heavy one in bringing about certain helpful changes. Recent years and particularly recent months have demonstrated, as we said in our report, "an impressive increase in restraint on the part of many news media organizations." This was discernible in our analysis of metropolitan newspapers, from responses to our questionnaires, and from the growing willingness of the media to subscribe to voluntary guidelines. Certain of them, the *Toledo Blade* and the Columbia Broadcasting System to cite two examples, set standards for themselves which were altogether laudable. It was noteworthy too that one strong big-city newspaper which thoroughly trounced us in its editorial columns in February within a matter of weeks thereafter issued to its reporters instructions on the handling of crime and court news to which no advocate of fair trial could object. So much has been and is being done. Much more can be when everyone becomes quite aware that this question of the news treatment of crime has needed a new look for a long, long time and that it will not be accompanied by as much pain as the Cassandras in the fourth estate have been prophesying.

Now we have taken a lot of advice, comment, and suggestion from the media. Some of it has been very good as I have indicated. The greater written part of it has, however, assumed the form of massive assault and, in too many more instances than I like to think about, it has been apparent to us that the authors simply have not plumbed the depths, and they are not too deep at that, of what we had to say. Consequently, reams of misinformation have reached the people and forward progress has been somewhat slowed. We are sorry about this. We expected better and were most willing to absorb press punishment on the assumption that it would take the form of accurate comment. Perhaps at this juncture it is not out of line and in the friendliest of spirits to offer the media some helpful suggestions. It strikes me that a great deal of the reporting of criminal matters is careless, imprecise, and inept. Since there is unquestionably a normal appetite and public curiosity, especially in these days, for news on crime, one of our four leading national problems, why does it not make sense that some real effort be made by the press to develop that competence among the men and women who cover crime news equal to that which leading newspapers have developed in specialized reporting on education, on advances in medicine, and on science in general? I do not mean to infer that there are not such reporters now working on crime news, for there are, but they seem few and far between. The impact of law and legal processes on the lives of everyone is such that I hope the news media will recognize the need of greatly increasing the number of qualified specialists in the field. Certainly, local bench and bar groups could assist in in-service training of such specialists that they might come up with that expert approach to the criminal story which marks the treatment by their fellows of what is being done in cancer laboratories and the colleges. Secondly, and this idea is not original with me, the media through their central organization should establish pooling arrangements for the notorious case which will prevent duplication of the shambles that was the Dallas courthouse in the hours following the presidential assassination. It is at such times that there is great strain on the whole structure of criminal justice and co-operation could do much to inhibit ghastly repetitions. Some signs of this cooperation have appeared and we need more.

The bench and the bar should also take a new tack. When the new ethical standard based on the rewrite of Canon 20 is officially promulgated it should be enforced. It will serve absolutely no purpose to have it on the books if it is to receive only token obeisance now and then as was the fate of its predecessor. It is not going to be easy to tighten the reins in many situations which I can visualize but the legal profession simply must call a halt to certain legal roughriders. Those gentlemen of the bar who employ press releases and press contacts as part of a field of maneuver for prosecution or defense should be curbed. Too often their peculiar forms of publicizing their cases, themselves, and their clients do disservice to the cause of justice, to the public, and to their own brothers in the profession. Their antics frequently disturb much more than the possibility of fair trial or the causes which command their attention from time to time.

Then there are the joint endeavors which remain for the media and the legal profession. Our committee now stands discharged and it has been succeeded by the Legal Advisory Committee recently appointed by the president of the American Bar Association to work out satisfactory press-bar liaisons all over the country. It is most desirable that the voluntary codes now operating with various degrees of success in an increasing number of states continue to grow in acceptance and strength. They will serve to complement our proposals and vice versa. The new committee can at the same time assist in keeping an eye on certain enforcement gentlemen here and there who may try to utilize our report as a shield for official activities which ought to be out in the open. It was never the intention of the committee to provide a barrier for such individuals who, of course, would resort to some other device or strategem were the report not in being.

Of equal importance is the positive necessity of continuing the dialogue between the men who are at the head of the media organizations and those who lead the organized and responsible bar. I see no need whatever of both parties standing off and unloading heavy barrages at each other. The conversations over the last three years have not produced full agreement to be sure but they have produced mutual respect. The collaboration which was possible even in disagreement should not be allowed to lapse. The coming months will prove that its continuance is vital if the accommodation which can be attained is to be achieved. This is an accommodation not only between the parties under law but is also that which will give full force to the guarantees of the First and Sixth Amendments, without those conflicts which have been deemed inevitable in many quarters.

We believe, as we have recommended, that this accommodation between the First and Sixth Amendments lies in the adoption of limitations—carefully defined as to content and timing—on the release of information bearing on the apprehension and trial of criminal defendants by members of the bar and by law enforcement agencies, with appropriate remedies available when there is a showing that a fair trial has been jeopardized. That is the succinct statement of what we have hammered out as a reasonable answer to the problem I have been discussing and I am satisfied that these recommendations, aimed as they are principally at cleaning up our own house, will stand the test of time and experience.

SECOND LECTURE

CLIFTON DANIEL

Perhaps I should begin this evening by congratulating Justice Reardon on his great victory in the House of Delegates of the American Bar Association last February. The House of Delegates overwhelmingly approved the Reardon Report—the report of the ABA Advisory Committee on Fair Trial and Free Press, of which Justice Reardon was chairman and David L. Shapiro was reporter.

As you already know, the report recommended very stringent new restrictions on the release of crime news to the press.

Specifically, it proposed a revision of the canon of professional ethics of the American legal profession, making it unethical for lawyers to release information or voice opinions that might prejudice a fair trial.

It recommended that similar restrictions be imposed on law enforcement agencies, judges and court officials, that pre-trial hearings be closed to the public, including the press, in certain circumstances, and that persons— obviously including newsmen—who disseminate information willfully designed to affect the outcome of a trial be punished for contempt of court.

These recommendations were adopted by the House of Delegates over the strenuous objections of representatives of the news media and without waiting for a study, sponsored by the American Newspaper Publishers Association, to determine whether pre-trial news really seriously affects the impartiality of juries.

Despite Justice Reardon's overwhelming victory, I am not entirely sure that congratulations are yet in order, that the press must yet concede defeat in its campaign against certain features of the Reardon Report.

First of all, the report was considerably watered down before it was even submitted to the American Bar Association. One of its most vindictive features was entirely eliminated—a proposal that fines imposed on newsmen for causing a mistrial be used to help defray the expenses of a new trial.

In the second place, while the Reardon Report has been approved by the national House of Delegates, it still has to be adopted by state and local bar associations—dozens of them—before it can have any restraining effect on the legal profession.

Some of the state associations, like the one in Kansas, have done nothing and are planning to do nothing. In Kansas, the Bar Association president told the Associated Press, "there is no enthusiasm for the Reardon Report."

Even if the stern restrictions of the Reardon Report are adopted by the bar associations, there is reason to wonder whether they will ever be effectively enforced by lawyers against their own kind.

The central feature of the report is simply an elaboration—more detailed and more specific—of one of the canons of professional ethics—Canon 20—that has been on the books for more than 50 years. Although Canon 20 is written in perfectly plain English, Justice Reardon says, "It has never been freighted with definite meaning, and it has never been enforced."

That is an extraordinary admission from a profession that writes most of our laws and purports to be qualified to administer them—an admission that for five decades it has been unable to write a rule of conduct for its own members that the profession—this learned profession—can understand and enforce.

According to Justice Reardon, there have been hundreds of cases in which the issue of prejudicial publicity was raised, but I have heard of only one action for disbarment against a lawyer for instigating, aiding and abetting the dissemination of prejudicial publicity. Remarkable!

Will this new canon be more rigidly enforced than the old one?

One wonders!

Justice Reardon says that the recommendations of his committee are aimed at putting the legal profession's house in order, not restricting the press.

One wonders about that as well!

Aside from the fact that the revised canon will have to be adopted and enforced by local bar associations, the Reardon committee's recommendations relating to the conduct of law enforcement offices will also have to be adopted by the police authorities in tens of thousands of separate jurisdictions, or by the courts in those jurisdictions, or the legislatures of the 50 states.

In the meantime, considerable doubt has been cast on the wisdom and even the constitutionality of this and other recommendations of the Reardon Report.

With all due respect to Justice Reardon, who is a distinguished member of the Massachusetts Supreme Judicial Court, jurists no less eminent than himself have publicly and emphatically disagreed with the Reardon Report.

One of those jurists is Judge Harold R. Medina of the United States Court of Appeals.

He was chairman of a special committee of the Association of the Bar of the City of New York, which presented a report last year closely parelleling the Reardon Report. But Judge Medina's committee dissented from the ABA recommendations on some very important points.

"Our conclusion," the committee said, "is that constitutional guarantees would stand in the way of most efforts to regulate the relationship between trials and the media, whether by legislation or by use of the contempt power."

At another point, the Medina committee said, "One of the conclusions reached by this committee is that because of the principles embedded in the First Amendment, the conduct of the press is largely beyond the control of the courts and the judges."

Then, in an interview last February, former Associate Justice Tom C. Clark of the United States Supreme Court said that the proposed new Bar Association rules were actually unnecessary. The courts, he said, already have sufficient power to prevent prejudicial publicity.

The Reardon Report, by imposing limits on statements by lawyers and the police and by barring newsmen from some court hearings could result in violations of freedom of the press, Justice Clark said.

"The Supreme Court," he added, "has been careful to protect the rights of the press, and I am satisfied it will continue to do so."

This was from the Supreme Court Justice who, while still on the bench, wrote the opinion in the Sheppard case—the case that gave so much impetus to the drive in the American Bar Association to impose restrictions on freedom of the press.

Last year, I was privileged to give testimony for three hours before a panel of seven federal judges, sitting in the Supreme Court Building in Washington, who were considering this free press-fair trial question.

Justice Clark addressed the panel for a few minutes, and I was honored when the Chief Justice himself came in and listened to me for a short while.

To my pleasure and surprise—and I think the judges were pleased and surprised as well—I found myself in substantial agreement with those distinguished jurists, headed by Judge Irving R. Kaufman of the United States Court of Appeals.

That panel, a committee of the United States Judicial Conference, appointed by the Chief Justice, has now proposed rules for press coverage of federal cases that would be far less restrictive than those of the Reardon Report. The committee considered and specifically rejected several measures recommended by Justice Reardon.

Let me read from the Federal Committee's report:

> The Committee does not presently recommend any direct curb or restraint on publication by the press of potentially prejudicial material. Such a curb, it feels, is both unwise as a matter of policy and poses serious constitutional problems. . . .

> Moreover, the Committee has decided not to make any recommendation at this time with respect to the exclusion of the press from preliminary hearings and other hearings held outside the presence of the jury. . . .

> The Committee also does not at this time recommend any judicially-imposed restrictions on the release of information by federal law enforcement agencies. The Committee is encouraged by the steps which have been taken by these agencies to set their own houses in order.

In other words, although Justice Reardon won an overwhelming victory in the House of Delegates, the action of the ABA is not final and conclusive. The ball game isn't over yet. It continues tonight and it will con-

tinue next week when Justice Reardon and I confront
each other at the National Press Club.

In my opinion, Justice Reardon and his colleagues are
using a sledgehammer to kill a gnat. Their heavy-handedness may wreck freedom of the press as well; it may
shatter the very keystone of our democracy.

Statistically speaking, the problem of prejudicial pre-
trial publicity is not of enormous dimensions.

Only a tiny fraction of criminal cases is ever reported
in the press, and in only a fraction of this fraction is
there any question of doing violence to the rights of
defendants.

In New York city, 11,724 felonies were committed in
January of 1965. Only 41 of those cases were mentioned
in the *Daily News,* and the *News* gives more attention
to crime than any other paper in town. If there were
violations of defendants' rights in any of the other
11,683 cases—and who can doubt that some violations
did occur—they cannot in any way be charged to the
newspapers.

"The more I study the Reardon Report, the more I
see it as a massive misdirected effort to solve a minor un-
defined problem by attacking it in the wrong places."

Those are the words of J. Edward Murray, managing
editor of the *Arizona Republic* and chairman of a committee of the American Society of Newspaper Editors
that waged a valiant but futile campaign against the
recommendations of the Reardon committee.

In fact, Mr. Murray said in a speech last year at the

University of Colorado, the problem of prejudicial pre-trial publicity is "so minor that only four cases involving it have been decided by the Supreme Court in twenty years, and one of these was an extraneous issue of television in the courtroom."

Even where pre-trial publicity becomes an issue, it is not a proven fact that publicity actually contaminates juries.

Take just one notorious case—the murder trial of Dr. Carl Coppolino in Freehold, New Jersey, the trial that preceded his conviction in Florida on another murder charge—a charge of murdering his wife.

Before Dr. Coppolino was brought to trial in Freehold, the most highly prejudicial information was printed about him in newspapers all over the country.

The Sunday before the trial started, *The New York Times Magazine* published an extremely laudatory article about Dr. Milton Helpern, the New York city medical examiner, who was to be one of the principal prosecution witnesses.

We received an indignant letter from one of our readers, saying that this article, which described Dr. Helpern as practically infallible, would make it impossible for Dr. Coppolino to get a fair trial in New Jersey.

In actual fact, the jury didn't believe Dr. Helpern's testimony, and, before I had time to reply to the reader's letter, Dr. Coppolino was acquitted.

The press was also acquitted, and so was the American jury system.

Sometimes I think we newspapermen have more faith in juries than lawyers have. Serving on a jury often brings out the best in a man. It may be the only time in his life when he is solemnly and publicly called upon to do his duty as a citizen. He takes his duty seriously, tries to clear his mind of prejudice, and render a fair judgment.

The juror who reads incriminating information about a defendant in his morning newspaper is just as likely to disbelieve the newspaper as he is to disbelieve the defendant—perhaps more likely.

Nowadays, there seems to be a notion that the ideal juror is an intellectual enuch, totally uninformed and blandly indifferent to his environment.

It was not ever thus—certainly not in the earlier, simpler days of our Republic, and in the small towns where I grew up.

In a small town, a man is tried by a jury of his peers —to wit, his neighbors. If the defendant happens to be the town drunk or a wife-beater, everybody knows it and the damaging facts are taken into account—as they should be.

I don't believe, and am sure you don't, that the Founding Fathers intended that jurors should be utterly empty-headed.

At least the Sixth Amendment says nothing to that

effect. "Impartial" is the word used in the Amendment, not "ignorant," or "uninformed."

Pre-trial publicity is, of course, not the only threat to that impartiality promised by the Sixth Amendment, and not the only source of prejudice in the minds of jurors.

There is a naive assumption in all this talk of prejudicial publicity that, if the newspapers did not publish it or the radio and television stations did not broadcast it, potential jurors would never hear it.

In fact, prejudicial publicity existed long before the invention of movable type. It was called gossip.

Word-of-mouth publicity is much more pervasive and virulent, much less accurate and precise than the written word in the hands of trained and responsible journalists.

Pre-trial publicity, whether printed, broadcast, or whispered over the back fence, is certainly not the most pressing issue in American jurisprudence today.

Let us not forget that the language of the Sixth Amendment calls for "a speedy and public trial by an impartial jury."

On this point, I like the vigor of Ed Murray's rhetoric so much that I want to quote him again.

> Although the long delay of cases in our court system is a well-publicized scandal, the Reardon Committee absolutely ignored the Constitution's requirement that trials be *speedy*.
>
> And the Committee is doing everything in its power to make trials less public.

The Committee *did* address itself to the need for impartial juries. But the main thrust of its work here has been to strengthen the unfortunate trend toward juries made up of citizens who are the least typical, the least informed, the least educated, and certainly the least equipped to deal intelligently and impartially with the growing complexities of the last third of the 20th century.

It seems to Mr. Murray and to me that the legal profession has become so obsessed with the problem of prejudicial publicity and so preoccupied with the rights of the individual—the criminal defendant—that it may lose sight of the public interest, the rights of society as a whole, the rights guaranteed in the First Amendment, including freedom of speech and freedom of the press.

Unless you've lived under a dictatorship, you can't appreciate the atmosphere of a country where the press is *not* free, where the newspapers never speak until spoken to.

I have lived in the Soviet Union. When I was there 13 years ago, it was possible for a man to be arrested without even his family knowing about it, much less his friends and his professional associates. He was simply missing. His family inquired, but his friends dared not do so, and his neighbors kept their doors locked, and listened at the keyhole.

The newspapers never reported his arrest. No hint of the charges against an ordinary citizen was ever given to the general public, even if he were brought to trial. The highest dignitaries of the state could disappear overnight, and nothing was heard of them until arrest, trial and execution were simultaneously announced in one terse communique.

Now, I know we are not talking here about instituting the Soviet system of justice—and that system itself is changing. But we should be talking about the abuses that can take place and do take place when the work of the police and the courts and the prisons is hidden from public view.

Until now, it has been the proud boast of American democracy that our press is free and our courts open to the public, to the end that justice will not merely be done, but will be *seen* to be done. Because of these freedoms, we hold our society to be superior to the dictatorships.

It is ironical that at the very moment when the American Bar Association is proposing to restrict crime news in the press and close some of our courtrooms to the public, people in the Communist countries have finally found the courage to cry out for freedom.

In Moscow, they demand admission to the courtrooms where political dissenters are in the dock. They smuggle out transcripts of secret trials.

In Warsaw they burn copies of the government newspapers because they know that the newspapers say only what the police and the censors permit them to say.

In Prague they finally publish accounts of political murders and purge trials long banned from the columns of the controlled press.

In the light of this very recent history, parts of the Reardon Report sound ominous indeed.

In that connection, I commend to you an article by John Hart Ely, published last year in *Encounter*. Mr. Ely was a member of the legal staff of the Warren Commission, a former law clerk to the Chief Justice of the United States, and is now on the staff of Defenders Incorporated in San Diego, California.

He spent a year in England gathering material for his article, and his thesis is this:

The "failure of American law to adopt the English contempt rule (as applied to pre-trial publicity) results not from lack of concern for the rights of defendants, but rather from a judgment deeply rooted in the American constitutional tradition: that by restricting what can be printed or broadcast about a criminal proceeding, a society loses many of the benefits deriving from a free press and is, therefore, better advised to enquire whether there aren't alternative means of safeguarding the right to a fair trial."

He reports that in the past the English press was of real assistance in investigating and uncovering crime, but, nowadays, most English editors take the view that the law's restrictions make exposure an activity too precarious to be undertaken.

Mr. Ely concludes, after examining both the British system and the American one, that "the only wholly satisfactory answer to the free press-trial problem is to find a way of leaving the press free to investigate and criticize—and at the same time insuring that the matter thus published will have no effect on the jury which ultimately tries the case."

He says, "It is this which the American system—albeit, to date, with a distinct lack of success—tries to do."

To remedy that lack of success, Mr. Ely advocates, first of all, applying more strenuously the remedies outlined in Justice Clark's opinion in the Sheppard case—that is, developing a set of procedural devices (and resuscitating old devices) that will insure the selection of a jury that has not been influenced by publicity. He says this system has not yet been given a real test.

"At present all we can say," Mr. Ely comments, "is what G. K. Chesterton said of Christianity: it 'has not been tried and found wanting. It has been found difficult, and left untried.'"

Mr. Ely concludes with something I first heard three or four years ago from Judge Skelly Wright of the Court of Appeals on the platform of the American Society of Newspaper Editors in Washington.

"Once in a while," Mr. Ely says, "there may arise a case so sensational that all the procedural devices in the world will not be able to guarantee the defendant a jury which has not been touched by publicity. In such a case, if the press is to be left free and the right to a fair trial preserved, the only alternative will be to let the defendant go free. The freeing of a man who may well be guilty is not a desirable occurrence. But if it is

the only way the two fundamental rights can be preserved, again, is it not worth the price?"

Or, as Justice Wright put it to me, "If you can't have
a fair trial, don't have a trial at all."

*   *   *

By this time, I can imagine you asking, "But isn't the
press going to do anything at all about this matter?"

My answer is that the press has done something, is
doing something, and will do something more.

First of all, its conscience has been stirred by the ac-
cusations of the Warren Commission and of the Supreme Court in the Sheppard case. But, before proceeding, let me say something about the Warren Commission.

I certainly would not argue that the manners of the
newspapermen, broadcasters, and photographers in
Dallas after the assassination of President Kennedy were
absolutely impeccable, but I do contend that the performance of the press in every other sense was superb.

I cannot recall a day in more than 30 years as a newspaperman when I was prouder of the product we were
able to give our readers than I was on the morning after
the President's assassination and in the days of mourning,
excitement, and introspection that followed.

We newspapermen and broadcasters served our clients
well. We kept the public informed, and kept the nation calm in an hour of grave anxiety and crisis.

And, what is more, within 48 hours, we reported the
Dallas story just about as accurately, if not as exhaus-

tively, as the Warren Commission did after ten months of work.

The Warren Commission said that in the atmosphere created in Dallas after the assassination it would have been impossible to give Lee Harvey Oswald a fair trial— if he had lived.

The commission then proceeded to give him a trial *in absentia* (and I think it was a fair one), while arguing that 12 good men and true could not have done the same thing.

Still, as I say, the Warren Commission and the Supreme Court have roused the conscience of the press.

I have never known the profession, collectively, to pay more serious attention to any ethical, legal or moral question or to study it more conscientiously.

The soul-searching has already had results. In 21 states the bar and the press have discussed guidelines for crime news coverage, and in nine of those states joint codes have been adopted.

Joint codes are under consideration in other states— Missouri, Oklahoma, New Mexico, Indiana, and Connecticut.

Individual newspapers and broadcasting companies have promulgated their own codes.

Many newspapers that have not committed their good intentions to paper have, nevertheless, been showing good intentions.

They are clearly more responsive to admonitions from

the bench and bar and clearly more restrained in their reporting of crime news than ever before.

In general, newspapers are changing in the direction of maturity, seriousness, responsibility, and sobriety.

A couple of years ago I attended a meeting with a group of business executives at the American Management Association. They complained that the press was not interested in constructive news, but was interested only in sex and sensation, crime and corruption.

One of them cited the way we were playing up the Miami murder case of Mrs. Candace Mossler and her nephew, which was then going on.

His allegation was a familiar one, but it didn't happen to be supported by the facts.

The facts were to be found in the February, 1966, issue of the *AP Log*, a weekly bulletin published by the Associated Press, which made a study of the way the Mossler case was being presented in the newspapers.

The study was based on an examination of 30 morning newspapers and 30 afternoon newspapers on a single day chosen at random. Those who examined the papers looked at 2,400 newspaper pages.

They found that of the 30 morning newspapers eight printed absolutely nothing about the Mossler case. Only four put the story on page 1. Most of the rest used short stories well back in the paper.

Of the 30 afternoon newspapers, 13 printed nothing. Only three put the story on page 1.

Summing up, the *AP Log* said, "The trial story is one

of the most sensational for some time, but with war and death on a grand scale, it appears the public doesn't care for crime news."

Any reader could confirm that by looking back at the newspapers published on the eight fateful days between the time that President Johnson announced his decision not to run for re-election and the funeral of the Rev. Dr. Martin Luther King.

Take another sensational case: there was clearly a new degree of restraint, dignity and sobriety in the reporting of the Speck case in Chicago—the case of Richard Speck, who was convicted of murdering eight student nurses.

You will recall that the trial judge tried to impose restrictions that the press considered excessive. The restrictions were challenged in a suit by the *Chicago Tribune* and they were then materially modified by the Illinois Supreme Court.

What was the result?

I quote from a report by William J. Conway, who covered the Speck trial for the Associated Press—the same man, incidentally, who, 34 years ago, wrote the Associated Press story on the death of John Dillinger.

Mr. Conway said of the Speck trial, "Newsmen exercised self-discipline above and beyond the judicial guidelines. . . . By the trial's end, there was a good relationship between the newsmen and Judge Paschen. The judge was on a first name basis with most of the 25 to 30 newsmen. Reporters spoke highly of the judge. Paschen in turn complimented the newsmen for their cooperation. Judge Paschen seemed to ignore many of the guidelines himself as the trial continued. . . .

"On the final day, Judge Paschen said from the bench: 'I thank the press for being well behaved.' "

The press was also well behaved in the second Sheppard trial.

The Supreme Court was quite right about the "massive, pervasive, and prejudicial" publicity that attended the original prosecution of Dr. Sam Sheppard. Whether or not he deserved to be acquitted, he certainly deserved a new trial.

But I am afraid we have forgotten where it all began and what purpose it was originally supposed to serve.

It began with a suspicion that somebody was "getting away with murder," and that the "somebody"—specifically, Dr. Sam Sheppard—was being protected by money, friendships and favoritism.

It began with a perfectly legitimate demand for an inquest and an arrest. The demand came from a newspaper with a conspicuous record of public service, the *Cleveland Press,* and an editor, Louis Seltzer, who was so greatly respected in his community that he was called "Mr. Cleveland."

We may concede that Mr. Seltzer's zeal was excessive, but could American democracy and American justice survive if editors like Louis Seltzer were effectively silenced by legislation and the courts?

Justice Reardon will tell you that the furthest thing

from his thoughts is silencing the press, that the new fair trial-free press standards are directed solely to lawyers and law enforcement agencies.

If that were strictly true, I would have no quarrel with the ABA.

More than three years ago, addressing the National District Attorneys Association in Houston, I said, "The press in general will interpose no objections to anything the bar, the bench and the police may do in the way of disciplining their own people, although we may feel constrained to point out the risks and evils in restricting the free flow of information to the public."

It is those risks and evils to which I have tried to address myself tonight.

One wonders what would have happened in Philadelphia, Mississippi, in the summer of 1964, if there had been no newspapermen—northern and southern newspapermen—prying into the disappearance of three civil rights workers there. Would the bodies ever have been found? Would anybody have been indicted for the murders? Would anybody ever have been convicted?

It isn't difficult to imagine the police in such a situation taking full advantage of a rule that allowed them —even encouraged them—to say practically nothing to the press.

It isn't difficult to imagine the courthouse gang in such a community arranging a secret hearing to dispose of an embarrassing case.

It isn't difficult to imagine a big-city, bought-and-paid-for judge and a corrupt prosecutor doing the same for a powerful politician.

It isn't difficult to imagine a judge opposed for re-election by a local newspaper threatening the editor with a contempt citation.

Nevertheless, I am confident that the American press will not be intimidated. Whatever the legal profession does, the press will not tamely submit to censorship by the police, lawyers, judges and legislators.

The press—and I mean newspapers, magazines, radio, and television—will do its duty. And, in so doing, it will serve not merely its own narrow interests but the cause of freedom, justice and democracy, and even the welfare of the bar and the bench, including, of course, Justice Reardon.

REBUTTALS

CLIFTON DANIEL

It is a pleasure for me to find myself at last on the same platform with Justice Reardon. This confrontation has been too long delayed.

We had a preliminary and private passage at arms more than a year ago. I was in Newport, Rhode Island, to address the New England Trial Judges Association, and at dinner I found myself seated two away from Justice Reardon.

Talking across the unfortunate guest who sat between us, we went at it hot and heavy while the roast beef was being served. I thought at the time that it would have been much more interesting for the audience if Justice Reardon and I had simply conducted our debate in front of the microphones, rather than my making a set speech.

Tonight, at long last, we have the microphones and an audience, and I, for one, am looking forward to the rest of the evening.

Many of you heard Justice Reardon's original presentation in this series two weeks ago. As I remarked last week when I made my own presentation, his remarks were certainly learned, clear and cogent, but, as you know, I was not entirely persuaded by them.

Tonight, there is not enough time for me to respond to every argument Justice Reardon made. So I will go directly to his conclusion.

"In the friendliest of spirits"—to use his words—Justice Reardon offered the news media "some helpful suggestions."

"It strikes me," he said, "that a great deal of the reporting on criminal matters is careless, imprecise and inept."

If I may say so, the Judge took the words right out of my mouth—only I would have applied them to the administration of justice in this country.

"Why," Justice Reardon went on, "does it not make sense that a real effort be made by the press to develop competence among the men and women who cover crime news equal to that which leading newspapers have developed in specialized reporting on education, on advances in medicine and on science in general."

It makes a great deal of sense, but Justice Reardon is a little late with his suggestion. Nearly 15 years ago, *The New York Times* sent Tony Lewis to Harvard on a Nieman Fellowship to study law in preparation for his assignment as the paper's Supreme Court reporter. I trust Justice Reardon will agree that the experiment was eminently successful.

If the reporting of legal matters in *The New York Times* is "careless, imprecise and inept"—which I do not admit for one minute—the legal profession must accept some of the blame.

Our present Supreme Court reporter and our principal writer on legal affairs in New York are both lawyers, and our reporter at police headquarters is a former secretary of the President's Crime Commission.

In fairness to Justice Reardon, I should say that he did not imply that no such reporters were now working on crime news, and he made the suggestion that "local bench and bar groups could assist in in-service training for such specialists."

Apparently, Justice Reardon wants to make little lawyers of us all. I can just imagine how a reporter might write a crime story after taking the Bar Association's course in gobbledygook and obfuscation:

> Two persons, one an adult male and the other an adult female (hereinafter called "the accused"), have been located together and in the same place by duly authorized officers and employes of the Police Department of the City of New York, while acting within the scope of their official employment, on or about 8:42 p.m. on the ninth day of May in the year 1968, on the premises at Eighth Avenue and West 41st Street, in the Borough of Manhattan, City, County and State of New York, said premises being more popularly known as the "Port of New York Authority Bus Terminal," said facility owned and operated by the Port of New York Authority, an agency established and existing by virtue of a compact entered into by and between the State of New York and New Jersey.
>
> At the time said event said male and said female were in the sole and exclusive possession of personal property, more particularly identified as one 1967

model motorbus, manufactured by the General Motors Corporation in or about the vicinity of Detroit, Michigan, and of which property the Greyhound Corporation, of New York City, was properly and lawfully seized.

The officers and employes of the Police Department of the City of New York, acting within their official capacity, accused, charged and complained that said adult male and said adult female committed and engaged in the crime—either felony or misdemeanor—of unlawfully and without proper cause or purpose appropriating said motorbus, complete with tankful of gasoline, to their own use, to wit: attempting and making an effort to operate, drive and abscond with said motorbus by means of egress from said Port of New York Authority Bus Terminal through the vehicular passageway more popularly known as the Lincoln Tunnel.

Until we learn the language of the law, we shall have to write the news in our simple, old-fashioned way:

A man and woman were arrested at the Port Authority Bus Terminal today on a charge of stealing a Greyhound Bus.

Speaking more seriously, Justice Reardon's idea of in-service training for crime news reporters isn't a bad one. It might be welcomed by the newspapers if presented to them in a friendly, helpful spirit. After all, lawyers have been addressing journalism classes, newspaper seminars and professional societies for more years than Justice Reardon and I can remember.

Another of Justice Reardon's proposals is equally acceptable—that "the media, through their central organizations, should establish pooling arrangements for the notorious case" that would prevent the sort of spectacle that occurred in Dallas after the assassination of President Kennedy.

I made a proposal to the same effect before the National District Attorneys Association in Houston more than three years ago.

I can heartily endorse also Justice Reardon's demand that when the new canon of ethics for the legal profession is promulgated, it should be enforced, making it unethical for lawyers to release information or voice opinions that might prejudice a fair trial. As Justice Reardon himself has often acknowledged, the existing canon, although written in perfectly plain English, "has never been enforced."

Indeed, discipline in the legal profession, on the testimony of former Justice Tom C. Clark, has been very lax in general.

According to a study made under his auspices in 13 states with about 80,000 lawyers, a total of 706 lawyers were professionally disciplined during the five years from 1962 to 1966. This is an average of 142 lawyers a year out of 80,000.

Certainly I can also agree with Justice Reardon in saying that the voluntary press and bar fair-trial codes now operating in a number of states should "continue to grow in acceptance and strength," and that the debate, discussion and collaboration between the press and the bar should continue.

What the press has been saying all along is that the restraints on pre-trial publicity should be voluntary and by agreement, not imposed on the press by the bar and the bench.

I don't want to leave the impression, however, that my endorsement of collaboration with the bar means that the press will tamely submit to the dictates of the American Bar Association, as expressed in the recommendations of Justice Reardon's committee adopted last February by the ABA House of Delegates.

I have to say that I deeply resent, and so do my colleagues, the repeated implication by spokesmen of the legal profession that journalism is a shoddy, money-grubbing business with no morals, no scruples, and no ethics.

We newspapermen do not believe that a law degree necessarily makes a man more honorable than a degree in journalism, or that elevation to the bench amounts to canonization.

I have absolutely no doubt that the free press in America has prevented and corrected far more injustices than it has committed.

This is not to say that the newspapers, magazines, radio, and television are without blame or blemish.

We of the press can readily admit that, in our zeal to publish, we sometimes do violence to the rights of defendants—unintentionally, inadvertently, without malice, but, nevertheless, deplorably.

Pre-trial publicity does, in a very small—indeed insignificant—number cases, make it difficult to conduct a fair trial. The press recognizes that fact and has been doing something about it, and is prepared to do a good deal more.

In the meantime, the press in general—magazines newspapers, radio and television—will interpose no objections to anything the bar, the bench and the police may do in the way of disciplining their own people, although we do feel constrained to point out the risks and evils of restricting the free flow of information to the public.

We must, in all conscience, resist those parts of the Reardon Report that would make legitimate news unavailable to the public, make trials more secret, and allow judges to dictate what the press might publish.

We believe that the presumptuous attempt of the American bar to prescribe rules of conduct not only for itself but also for the police and the press is unwise, unhelpful, unlikely to be effective, and is, in all probability, unconstitutional.

PAUL C. REARDON

Two weeks ago this evening I appeared here in Washington in the first of three meetings devoted to what is denominated a "Rational Debate Seminar" on the subject of Fair Trial-Free Press. At that time I indicated that there *was* a problem in accommodating the guarantees of the First and Sixth Amendments, that it seemed to me there was a general recognition of the fact that this problem did exist, and that a committee which I was privileged to head had been trying to do something about it. I mentioned the impetus which had been given to our studies by the Warren Report, as well indeed by the sentiment of large numbers of American trial judges, that here was a dilemma which required solution. I stated that it was not one of recent origin, that it had been with us for a long, long time. I further stated that our contacts with the heads of organizations representing the American news media had produced a common accord that, in truth, the specter of pre-trial prejudicial publicity as well as damaging publicity during ongoing jury trials was with us. There is no necessity of reviewing examples of it such as those published in our report. Suffice it to say that prejudicial publicity has marred the conduct of altogether too many American trials. I described the study which the committee had undertaken, what we had done, where we had gone, and the conclusions which we had reached. Our researches, over three years, were most extensive, were carefully carried out and pursued with an impartial objectivity. I suggest that a detached observer, regarding and weighing their results, would consider that there had been a fair review and analysis of the mass of material we considered. I regret only that this evening's audience has not been able to hear in extenso exactly what it was that we surveyed and how it was that we arrived at our conclusions. Limits of time do not allow tonight a repetition of what was said two weeks ago. However, I can capsule our recommendations.

Our committee has held that the accommodation between the First and Sixth Amendments lies in the adoption of limitations—carefully defined as to content and timing—on the release of information bearing on the apprehension and trial of criminal defendants by members of the bar and by law enforcement agencies with appropriate remedies available when there is a showing that fair trial has been jeopardized. Translated, our recommendations, which mirror the concept I have just expressed, thrust mainly at lawyers as officers of the court and the enforcement agencies. We have suggested certain standards which in affect will serve as a guide to those most closely allied with the work of the courts as to what they should and should not say relative to investigations, indictments, and ongoing trials. In short, our standards represent an honest endeavor to straighten out within our own house situations stemming from prejudicial pre-trial publicity which have represented, in our view, a threat to the Sixth Amendment guarantees. These proposals do not contravene the guarantees of the First Amendment. Relative to those guarantees our standards are not intended to and do not inhibit in any way the ability of the news media to publish all they will about crime, court administration, corruption in public affairs, or in any matter developed by the media through their own investigation or initiative. I pause only to comment that what the standards do not suggest or do not do has been little recognized or discussed by the media since those standards were first published.

Based upon that very brief outline of my original presentation I should like to proceed to a consideration of the paper which Mr. Daniel presented last week. I propose to deal with certain arguments he adduced in that paper seriatim. Since most of you were not present when he delivered it, I am under some necessity of telling you what he said and what I think about it.

First of all, although I think with tongue in cheek, Mr. Daniel congratulated me for an "overwhelming victory" in that the Bar Association accepted our recommendations in Chicago in February. The manner in which he phrased his congratulations leads me to say in all seriousness that we have never in three and a half years of work on this study thought in terms of victory or winning anything at all. This discussion is not a question of winning a battle. It is rather a question of the opportunity for all good citizens, in the media, on the bench, or at the bar, to move along together to settle the differences which exist in the Fair Trial-Free Press area that the administration of criminal justice may be strengthened. I thus with respect decline to accept Mr. Daniel's congratulations.

Secondly, he pointed to the lack of enforcement of Canon 20, which is the present canon dealing with these matters, and prognosticated that the new canon will not be enforced. Of course what we have tried to do is to clarify and strengthened the language of the old canon. Strangely enough the old canon seems satisfactory to the media. That it is satisfactory lies in its lack of enforcement. That it has not received enforcement lies in the vagueness of its language. I suggest that we have straightened out the language and that the new standard presents a readily enforceable guide. I therefore conclude that the dislike of Mr. Daniel and others who support his view of the new standard springs from an inner desire that no standards in this area be enforced at all.

Thirdly, my friend from the *Times* called to his aid judicial expressions of opinion which diverge, as he sees it, from our conclusions. It is perfectly true that there has been some divergence but our committee considers it to be minor. As a matter of fact, Mr. Daniel attempts to make much out of certain differences in the report on this subject of the federal judges which is going to be considered by the entire federal judiciary presently. When the tentative report of the federal judges was issued a short time ago and the press set about spotlighting these differences, Judge Kaufman, the chairman of the Federal Judges Committee, wrote a letter to Mr. Daniel's newspaper in which he quite properly pointed out that the attention of his committee was principally directed "at the Free Press-Fair Trial dilemma as manifested in the Federal courts." He continued, "As we attempted to make clear in our report, the problem in the state courts to which the Reardon report also addressed itself is of a somewhat different nature." As a matter of fact the tentative draft for the federal judges is extremely close to our report in the most important features of both. The federal judges' report recommends adoption of our revised canon. The present restrictions of the Department of Justice on release of pre-trial publicity parallel ours save in one respect and thus there was no need for the federal judges to do more in that area. The mandates of the Sheppard case relative to the conduct of a trial are already in being. Parenthetically, may I say that Mr. Daniel is in error when he alleged last week that the Sheppard case provided "so much impetus to the drive in the American Bar Association to impose restrictions on the freedom of the press." We commenced our work in late 1964. *Sheppard* v. *Maxwell* came down on June 6, 1966. In any event, I assume Mr.

Daniel has no debate with the requirements of that case relative to the conduct of a trial which are so closely similar to our own.

Fourthly, Mr. Daniel has stated that "Justice Reardon and his colleagues are using a sledge hammer to kill a gnat." I find myself in disagreement with that statement. Our report has indicated the scope of this problem. It exists. That the cases which concern us are small percentagewise although not few in number does not detract from their importance because, as has been said elsewhere, it is these "that test the very fabric of our judicial system by placing the most stress upon it." If Mr. Daniel does not recognize the existence of this problem I can give him the names of a dozen of his most noted colleagues around the United States who have agreed with us that it does exist.

Fifthly, my friend asserted when he was here last week "that the legal profession has become so obsessed with the problem of prejudicial pre-trial publicity and so preoccupied with the rights of the individual—the criminal defendant—that it may lose sight of the public interest, the rights of society as a whole, the rights guaranteed in the First Amendment including freedom of speech and freedom of the press." It seems to me that in this observation he overlooks two important facts. The first is that in drafting our standards we have tried not to make it any easier for the criminal defendant. The reverse is true. What we have endeavored to do is to lessen the possibility of reversals of convictions of a goodly number of crooks who ramble about our society on the grounds that their causes were prejudiced by publicity about them. We desire to make convictions stick. I have at hand some examples from Mr. Daniel's paper which will amply demonstrate the difficulty. Again, the study which our committee made constituted one of a set of six massive studies in problems dealing with the administration of criminal justice. I have not seen the American media paying much attention to those studies which are every bit as important as our own, and the simple reason for this is that they do not involve the areas which are closest to the hearts of the media. So I dislike to hear from Mr. Daniel that this problem of prejudicial publicity is an obsession with us. I suggest with all respect that any incipient psychoses on the subject are to be found among the media rather than with the bench and the bar. I further suggest, although he doesn't give us credit in his paper, that the conscience of the press has had some assistance from what we have been doing. If the whole debate were to cease right now a great deal of progress has been made. We recognize it, and modestly I claim that we had something to do with it.

There is much more that I could say about Mr. Daniel's paper, with certain points of which I am in agreement. I can only conclude, however, that our committee tried to do its job well, that it accepted solid suggestion from all quarters including the media, that it makes no apology for its product, that that product is going to be around for quite awhile, and that the cause of criminal justice will be better served in the long run if we endeavor to pull together, keep the dialogue going, and, as *The New York Times* itself recently suggested, "play it cool."

DISCUSSION

FIRST SESSION

WALTER GARVER, U. S. Chamber of Commerce: Much of the problem between the press and the courts and the bar in fact stems from the need for accommodation between the necessities of each? For the press, I'd say 90 percent or more of the media's commodity is time and making deadlines. I've had financial and business reporters come to me for background on a story where they thought I had it but they couldn't spend long enough to get to the bottom of the thing and understand it. They had to go write another story.

On the other hand jurists and the bar are concerned with making a record which will stand for all time—it is said that the wheels of justice grind slowly but exceedingly fine. In other words, the bar and the press are at opposite poles on the importance of time—a weakness on both sides, so to speak, with weakness in quotation marks, in conflict here.

He perhaps wants a story for the deadline of an edition but justice has to take its time and be sure that it is thoroughly done. Isn't a good share of the difficulty this kind of opposite poles of motivation?

JUSTICE REARDON: I have no doubt that that is so. I have no doubt that there are other questions of press operation with which we of necessity must be very unfamiliar, problems which the press has to meet daily which we just don't know about. I think the press could perhaps take the view that it has not had a fair shake in a consideration of those problems.

Secondly, in this provision for the closing of preliminary hearings on rare occasions, there is a feeling that, even though a record is transcribed and kept, the news from the preliminary hearing is stale by the time it is released. That is a problem of press operation, which we recognize to exist.

I think I am right in saying that at the conclusion of the Speck trial there were released on the day of sentencing by Judge [Herbert C.] Paschen in Peoria two statements made by Speck while in custody. These were, for one reason or another, inadmissible at the time of trial. I saw those reported only in *The New York Times*. In these statements Speck most definitely implicated himself. The reason for their exclusion I do not know. But that is an example of the second phase of the problem.

LUTHER HUSTON, *Editor and Publisher:* Justice Reardon, are you aware of a petition for *certiorari* which was filed just a few days ago in the Supreme Court to test the discretionary authority of the judge at a preliminary hearing to declare the hearing closed or open?

JUSTICE REARDON: Yes, I am.

MR. HUSTON: The Arizona case?

JUSTICE REARDON: Yes.

MR. HUSTON: Won't that present a rather important question to the Supreme Court, if they decide to hear it?

JUSTICE REARDON: It could present an important question bearing on matters that we have considered.

JOHN P. MacKENZIE, *Washington Post:* Justice Reardon, I don't understand why there will be so few preliminary hearings that are closed temporarily. I think the standards say that they shall be closed on the request of the defendant unless the judge determines—and then there is a list of things that he must determine. It doesn't seem to me very discretionary for the trial judge.

JUSTICE REARDON: I disagree. The closure of the *voir dire* or the preliminary hearing is at the discretion of the judge upon request. As a practical matter, based on my own experience in a jurisdiction which has closed such hearings for many years, if that discretion is properly exercised the closures will be more rare than otherwise.

I would like to speak a minute on this closure. What bothered us, of course, was inadmissible material coming in which would prejudice the jury, which is not sequestered in most jurisdictions. In Massachusetts we sequester juries, of course, on capital cases. In fact, in the top of our courthouse in Boston we have a hotel for them. Jurors are locked up on every capital case in Massachu-

setts; that's always been so. Many of the problems which
bedevil states where that is not so do not bedevil us.
Such problems do arise to bedevil one when the case is
a long one and when one cannot sequester a jury. We've
got a case in Massachusetts now, involving small loans
transactions, which has been running ten or 11 months.
Of course, you can't lock up a jury for that course of
time. But, as a practical matter, closures with us have
been rare.

When we reached this problem of how to protect the
juror from reading when he goes home at night what
he was not supposed to hear during the daytime, we
considered a number of states which, either as in our
case did this traditionally, without statutory mandate,
or under a New York law of some 80 years ago, em-
powered the judge to close preliminary hearings. There
are five or six state statutes which empower judges now
to do just this. This Arizona case of which Mr. Huston
speaks has to do with some goings on in Arizona. They
had the law there and I think they have since repealed it.

MR. HUSTON: The Supreme Court of Arizona repealed it.

JUSTICE REARDON: That's right. That was a
decision by Chief Justice Bernstein down there, I think,
on that. Here we had a ready-made answer in half a
dozen states to this particular problem. Now, I suggest
to you, on the basis of my own experience with trial
courts, which is limited but nonetheless it is that of an
average judge, that the proper exercise of discretion by

the trial judge, given the power to close, will be employed with great care.

MR. MacKENZIE: Is the word discretion anywhere in that standard?

JUSTICE REARDON: I can just read it to you: "The hearing may be closed if there are matters that will be inadmissible as evidence at the trial and it is therefore likely to interfere with his right to a fair trial by an impartial jury. The motion shall be granted unless the presiding officer determines that there is no substantial likelihood of such interference," for which I substitute the word discretion.

MR. MacKENZIE: They could have said it plainer than that if they meant "discretionary."

RUSSELL FREEBURG, *Chicago Tribune:* Justice Reardon, on this point, I have here a clipping from last August which says the Second District Court of Appeals in California struck down a Los Angeles Superior Court Order on the pretrial hearing. The clipping states that this might be counter to the Fourteenth Amendment, which you haven't mentioned at all. What are your views on this?

JUSTICE REARDON: Where is that case right now?

MR. FREEBURG: I don't know.

JUSTICE REARDON: That was the case involving Judge Smith in Los Angeles, I believe, was it not, who issued a blanket order against the Los Angeles county enforcement officials. I would not want to comment on that case.

MR. HUSTON: Of course, this Arizona case was heard by the Ninth Circuit Court.

JUSTICE REARDON: Yes.

MR. HUSTON: Then this might be what you're talking about?

JUSTICE REARDON: This is a different case. This is an earlier case. There was a blanket order issued by one of the 130 superior court judges in the county of Los Angeles.

MR. FREEBURG: Could I take a hypothetical case then and ask: Would the pre-trial period go counter to the Fourteenth Amendment, which is what, the due process of law? Might it?

JUSTICE REARDON: If your question is whether these recommendations apply into the pre-trial period, it is our intention so to apply them.

THEODORE PIERSON, lawyer representing Radio, Television News Directors Association: If you will recall, during the several conferences that we had in several parts of the country, one of our objections was that you really made it a presumption of prejudice if the defendant raised the question with respect to a preliminary hearing; that unless the judge found that there would be no prejudice, he had to grant the motion.

We suggested that it ought to be the other way around: that the judge would have to find that there was a clear and present danger or a substantial likelihood of prejudice before he would grant the motion. We made that suggestion about three times. Every time it was rejected. I submit that the way that provision is worded the judge has little discretion, unless the evidence before him establishes beyond a peradventure of a doubt that there will not be prejudice. I think his discretion is very limited and I think that most trial judges will follow that pattern.

JUSTICE REARDON: The language says that the motion shall be granted unless the presiding officer determines that there is "no substantial likelihood," those words are in there, of such interference.

MR. PIERSON: Right. It says it shall be granted. We have suggested that the motion shall be granted if the judge determines that there is a clear and present danger to the fair trial. There is a vast difference between those.

JUSTICE REARDON: Yes.

MR. PIERSON: One is the presumption that there will be [prejudice] going in, unless whoever represents the press, and I don't know who does in these circumstances, proves that negative. We felt that the defendant ought to be required to prove that there is a substantial likelihood of prejudice.

JUSTICE REARDON: I remember—

MR. PIERSON: But we had deaf ears turned to this. You recall that.

JUSTICE REARDON: We heard you.

MR. PIERSON: Yes, you did. [Laughter.]

PAUL CONRAD, National Newspaper Association: Following along on this area of closing the trial, this rather assumes, does it not, that the jurors are likely to read or hear press coverage of the trial.

JUSTICE REARDON: It is more than an assumption. We've got plenty of documentation in the cases that they do and have.

MR. CONRAD: Doesn't this create an almost impossible situation when it comes to public trials? This puts the whole system then at the mercy of the reporter, whether he does his job well. He can make an error or he can present one side of the day's trial and thereby create a possibility of prejudice, even if there is nothing that justifies the closing of that day's hearing.

JUSTICE REARDON: Are you speaking about preliminary hearings?

MR. CONRAD: No, no, the trial itself, during the course of the trial, where you are closing the trial because something is going to be brought out outside of the presence of the jury.

JUSTICE REARDON: That is a *voir dire* on a confession or something of the sort?

MR. CONRAD: Yes.

JUSTICE REARDON: I suggest to you that the average case on the closing of a *voir dire* gives some indication that a confession is about to be introduced. There is an objection on the basis that there was something faulty with the taking of the confession, a failure to warn or something of the sort. The judge will have to determine this, under our practice, first. The jury is sent out and the judge takes evidence on the confession, how it was obtained, the circumstances and the rest. He then decides to admit the confession, or exclude it. Assuming he takes the first course and the confession is admitted, when everybody comes back into the court-room presently, the jury, the reporter, and anyone else in the courtroom is going to hear that confession. Assuming that he excludes it, all of the material that will have been placed before him in the hearing is retained in the transcript subject to subsequent disclosure.

Now, I suggest to you that the average case by a competent trial judge will embody very, very few of those close-downs, very, very few. If the confession is admitted there is no press difficulty at all. If it is excluded, the minute the sentence is passed out the confession and everything that has been taken down is released.

I frankly fail to see what the worries are on this closure, except in the case of the judge who over-reacts to every piece of evidence coming along and says, "Well, I'm going to fire everyone out of this courtroom till I pass on this, that or the other thing." There is nothing in our recommendations that warrants any such conduct.

MR. MacKENZIE: There is nothing in the recommendations that tells the trial judge not to behave that way either.

JUSTICE REARDON: No. There are some 3,500 jury trial judges in this country and I disagree with Mr. Howard James on the competence of the American trial judge. I know hundreds of them and many of these men are taking training a month at a time now. Mr. Justice

[Tom] Clark, and the whole country should be grateful to him for it, has set up these schools for collegiate training of judges. They are working at it. I don't take the dim view of the American judge that Mr. Howard James does. I think that in these situations the defendant, the press and the public are going to come off well enough.

MR. MacKENZIE: It is not just a matter of competence; it's a mater of guidelines for the judge. You're setting standards here.

JUSTICE REARDON: Yes, I know, but you can't go all the way down the line on every jot and tittle. What you are trying to do is set up a general, recommended set of operations and assume that the trial judiciary of the United States is going to exercise its corporate brains. I think they have them.

THEODORE McDOWELL, *Washington Star* Broadcasting Company: Judge Reardon, I would like to look ahead a moment with a question regarding a story that moved on May 1 on the wire. It says: "the American Bar Association said today its Committee on Fair Trial and Free Press will encourage bar groups and the news media to draw up voluntary codes which include the substance of the ABA fair trial-free press standards."

It goes on to say that the validity of voluntary codes obviously will depend on how successful they prove to be in accomplishing their objectives. Isn't this really a piecemeal adoption, state by state and jurisdiction by jurisdiction, *in toto* of the recommendations that were adopted by the ABA?

There are hookers in here which indicate to me that if a local press-and-bar group doesn't go as far as the ABA rules it would be overruled and the rules would then be set by the courts.

JUSTICE REARDON: I would answer that broadly by saying this: When our committee was discharged in February this second committee came into being. It is headed by Chief Judge Devitt of Minnesota. It has a distinguished membership, including a gentleman present in the room here, Mr. Anello over there, the general counsel for the National Association of Broadcasters.

The theory and thought behind this committee, is that it will pick up and attempt to develop voluntary codes through the states with the press. Anything that we have recommended or any action that the Bar Association took in Chicago will serve only, it seems to us, to strengthen and to complement those codes.

There are no hookers. What we have endeavored to do here is to go after our own barristers and the enforcement people, to try to tell them to be a little more cautious in this field. Certainly most press-bar codes seem to try to do the same things for both press and bar in the respective states. Not all of them accomplish it. Some of these codes have exceptions, but I don't see any booby-traps.

MR. McDOWELL: It says here, for instance, that "ultimately the decision will rest with the court in each jurisdiction, whether it is necessary or not necessary in the light of experience, to apply the ABA standards by rule of the court."

Doesn't that really mean that if we get together here in the District, for instance, and come up with something, that doesn't go the full way toward the ABA recommendations the court is going to say anyway, "Let's adopt the ABA standards"?

JUSTICE REARDON: I can't prognosticate on that because there are 50 different situations around the United States. I would say this on the press-bar codes. To the extent that those are implemented and abided by, to that extent it would be less necessary to resort to these recommendations. The trouble with the codes, as I see them, is that almost all of them have an escape hatch. If you cannot catch the notorious case within the web of a press-bar code, then that code, I suggest, is not much good. And when a press-bar code lays down certain guidelines and then contains a series of exceptions it isn't a code. It isn't a working code. That's one of the problems.

The second problem we ran into is that there are certain newspapers in this United States which are never going to subscribe to codes anyway. We have written evidence of that.

This new committee is going to try and work to get the codes in being around the country and to strengthen them. I would further say that there is nothing in our recommendations that should inhibit that development.

MR. McDOWELL: Let me ask you one further question, sir. You mentioned, I believe, a CBS code.

JUSTICE REARDON: Yes.

MR. McDOWELL: Which, if I recall correctly, is taken directly from the [then Attorney General Nicholas] Katzenbach rules laid down several years ago, is it not? Many news organizations on their own have adopted in whole or part those Katzenbach recommendations, including my organization. But that is within our shop, without agreement with anybody else. Would you consider that the Katzenbach recommendations meet the needs that we are discussing here?

JUSTICE REARDON: I think the Katzenbach recommendations are on a complete par with ours insofar as the rules that were laid down for the Department [of Justice] are concerned, with the sole exception of prior criminal records. That is the one place that we parted. In rereading them prior to coming down here I found that he stated, on records, that there remains substantial feeling within the department that even this solution to the question of disclosing prior records is too permissive. In other words, in the address announcing his recommendations to the American Society of Newspaper Editors, in April of 1965, he set out standards for the department which are almost on a par with ours, save for this item of publication of records.

MR. McDOWELL: What was his statement on records, that in certain cases they could be disclosed?

JUSTICE REARDON: That's right. But he has indicated that there was feeling in the department that the department was too permissive and we think the department is.

MR. PIERSON: Also, Judge Reardon, didn't they reserve discretion to the attorney general to make any further public announcements that the attorney general decided were appropriate?

JUSTICE REARDON: I can't remember, Mr. Pierson. It may well be so.

MR. PIERSON: There was discretion in the executive agencies that wasn't restricted by any judicial order. I am somewhat interested in your remarks that unless these proposed rules can take care of the notorious cases they haven't accomplished a thing.

Assume the current American Bar Association proposals were in effect at the time of the Kennedy assassination, when the whole country was terribly shocked, many of them in panic as to whether this was some kind of conspiracy to kill all of the executive officers of government, widely concerned about whether this was the beginning of the end of something. Is it conceivable that the law enforcement agencies involved, the Dallas police, the Federal Bureau of Investigation, the Secret Service, possibly could have limited the information that they released to what your report recommends?

JUSTICE REARDON: All I can say is that we had one member on our committee from Dallas. He was in on large segments of that situation down there. There is no question that cables ran through that courthouse—

MR. PIERSON: I'm not talking about the disorder, Judge Reardon. I'm talking about whether the country would have been satisfied on publication of arrest and charge, the identity, that he was married, and his residence. Would we have waited six or eight months or 12 months before the country would have found out that this presumably was the act of an individual person?

JUSTICE REARDON: I think that under these recommendations enough could have been said to have allayed public apprehension and at the same time give him a fair trial. It's as certain as I sit here that he never could have received a fair trial anywhere in the United States.

MR. PIERSON: I think that maybe we can concede that. I am just saying that the interest of the country was in being certain that this was the act of an insane individual, that it was not some Communist conspiracy or right-wing conspiracy. Could the country have waited, under any kind of rule that you have, to get that information at the time of the trial?

You have attended a number of our meetings—

JUSTICE REARDON: Yes.

MR. PIERSON: —and I have been circumspect, as I think we all were, in any disclosures as to what went on there. But I think it is safe enough to say that there was a body of feeling that there are certain cases in which there never can be a fair trial; that in cases of tremendous public moment such as that, the right of the public to the information outweighs any rights that the defendant may have.

JUSTICE REARDON: These are the notorious cases.

MR. PIERSON: Those are the notorious cases.

JUSTICE REARDON: That theory can be argued on both sides. You have just argued it on one side. We are in complete and utter disagreement on this point. These notorious cases most severely test our fabric, put it to its toughest test. We simply must strive, whether we achieve it or not, to make certain that the type of events that followed the Kennedy assassination do not happen again.

Why cannot there be enough in the way of a release to the public in that case, whether it be that case or the Speck case, without having some of the incidents occur which occurred relative to both cases, allaying public apprehension and at the same time giving the miserable wretch who is in the middle the trial he is entitled to?

MR. PIERSON: If we assume that the information released by the Dallas police and the federal officials was limited to what the Reardon Report recommendations would permit, I venture to suggest that the media of the country would find other means to satisfy this insatiable and insistent demand of the public to know what happened and what was back of this. They would largely be dealing with rumor and gossip. They wouldn't be able to get from the law enforcement agencies accurate facts. I would suspect that there would have been no dearth of theories about what was behind the assassination of Kennedy if the police were muzzled. As a matter of fact, I think much more damage could have resulted if the police had been muzzled.

JUSTICE REARDON: All right. After the Oswald murder or after the Kennedy assassination, all the rules were down, everybody was in there, there was plenty of talk. The public got every last bit of information that it could have procured under any circumstances. But right now today you have a half a dozen theories that are being detailed in hardback books by gentlemen who are still belaboring the issues. So I don't think you prove a thing when you make a statement like that, Mr. Pierson, I really don't.

MR. PIERSON: The only statement I am making right now, Judge Reardon, is that by muzzling the people who do have the facts, who can give accurate information to the public, you do not necessarily prevent all kinds of publications about what happened based on inaccurate facts.

JUSTICE REARDON: That is true and that is a problem for the press. If the press endeavors to do within its own field what we have endeavored to do in ours, a lot of these situations which give us trouble might be resolved.

MR. CONRAD: You say if the notorious case can't be handled then we haven't achieved the goal. The Reardon recommendations provide for the situation in which the person is not yet apprehended. In those situations material can be released which otherwise would not be available, prior criminal records, probative information, all of the things that it might take to bring that person into custody. We have this example in the person who presumably has assassinated Martin Luther King, Mr. Ray Gault or whatever his name may be.

JUSTICE REARDON: We certainly do.

MR. CONRAD: Don't you have the seeds of destruction of your own recommendation right there? That information has been made available within the terms of the Reardon recommendation and yet we still have to face the problem of trying the man if he is ever apprehended.

JUSTICE REARDON: That is all very well but what I tried to say initially is that the main thrust of these recommendations—and the public hasn't been told this, I suggest, to any great extent—is against the lawyers and the law enforcement agencies, the people over whom we have some control, who can be subject to some professional discipline within our own house. It is perfectly true that on a notorious case the large newspaper or publications or combines can send fleets of investigators into the field to blanket the investigative forces of a great many communities. That's a problem we cannot touch. We do not attempt to reach it. We have not in any way inhibited the press from doing just that. That is the press' problem and that is a problem which, in view of things that have been going on lately, I suggest the press ought to be thinking about instead of belaboring us for endeavoring to clean up our own houses.

MR. CONRAD: Yes, but the information has come

from the law enforcement agencies in this case, the fingerprints to indicate how the authorities happen to think that Gault is involved. That information has come from the law enforcement agencies. They have not violated your recommendations, have they?

JUSTICE REARDON: I would not want to comment, Mr. Conrad, on that situation. I'm aware of it, but that's a very live situation and that is a case that is not yet brought to trial. I am just speaking in generalities, which I think is much safer.

MR. PIERSON: Judge Reardon, is there any part of your recommendation which would restrain an officer of the court or a law enforcement officer from making a statement, in a complicated situation such as the Kennedy assassination, that there was no information in the hands of the officials which indicated a wide conspiracy or that implicated any individual other than the person currently charged with the crime, and letting it go at that?

JUSTICE REARDON: If you will just pardon me for a minute while I read some of my own recommendations. [Laughter.] I would think that it might be all right, under these recommendations, to make that statement prior to the apprehension of a suspect. With respect to a grand jury or the pending investigation of a criminal matter, that includes apprehension of a suspect, a lawyer, a district attorney shall not make any such extrajudicial statement beyond the public record that is not necessary to inform the public that the investigation is under way or to describe the general scope of the investigation. I would think that would be all right.

MR. McDOWELL: Really, you can't govern the problem just by dealing mainly with the bar. Actually the ABA should also have recommended perhaps far wider use of the contempt power to deal with the press, particularly where they do deal in the realm of rumor.

JUSTICE REARDON: There are those on the committee who thought we should do that. If we have narrowed the scope of the contempt power—and I believe it is narrower than that which inherently lies in the court —we narrowed it on the grounds that I indicated previously, that we were trying to come as close as we could to the press in the hopes of a joint statement. If there was any theory of logic or any basis for what happened, that was it.

MR. HUSTON: Do you think there would be any merit or virtue in every judge having a press relations officer?

JUDGE REARDON: Quite a few of them have already, Mr. Huston, I think. [Laughter.] I don't think so. I think that there are all sorts of complications here with elected judges and elected prosecutors and the rest. We don't have the problem in Massachusetts because we are appointed for life. We don't have elected judges.

Conditions for the elected judge are quite different, I fully understand and recognize on behalf of those of us who enjoy life tenure for good behavior. The public is best served not by a judge handing out press releases. The public is best served by the competent reporter in the judge's court room. And when I say competent reporter, I mean competent in the sense that he is a specialist in that type of reporting. So my answer to that question would be in the negative.

MR. PIERSON: A couple of times, Mr. Justice, you mentioned the efforts to have a joint statement. I am curious to know if you thought the situation was so critical or so urgent that it required your going it alone. Why did you abandon the efforts to have a joint statement?

JUSTICE REARDON: Because it became perfectly clear on October 2, 1966, when we released this report, that we would never get it. We were hit by every newspaper in the country with the exception of about ten, and I can name them for you. I found that it would be almost completely impossible to have a meeting of the minds on these matters—just by reading, as I did, what came from around the United States.

MR. PIERSON: Do you judge that the attitude on the part of the press or all media is harder now than it was at that time, or softer?

JUSTICE REARDON: I don't think it's any softer.

MR. PIERSON: Then haven't you polarized the feeling and haven't you really closed the door now on any possibility?

Outside of your judgment that you couldn't get agreement, which I believe somewhat of a judgment, I suppose, was it not worth it to attempt it? It seems to me now that it's like a divorce. The effort at reconciliation seems terribly remote now.

JUSTICE REARDON: I don't think that's necessarily so. There was a feeling after the action in Chicago, among some of the states that are affected by the code's working, of some dismay and some indignation. But I see no reason why these colloquies and dialogues between the media and the bench and bar should not continue. But once we determined that we could not have a meeting of the minds, it seemed to me that that was the point to resolve to move forward and at least clean up that area of the bar which was in our charge. That's what we did.

MR. PIERSON: Did you have a reading from the media that they felt, as well, that this issue could not be resolved?

JUSTICE REARDON: I had the distinct impression that they would not agree with our incursions into areas of enforcement, for instance on the preliminary hearings that have been discussed.

A VOICE: Well, I did ask for a year's delay.

JUSTICE REARDON: Yes, that is true. But I don't think the year's delay, as I said at Chicago, would have made the slightest bit of difference. And I stated at Chicago why.

MR. MacKENZIE: I think I ought to say that I didn't think much of the motion for delay on the basis of the study. But what was the decision of the committee in 1964 as to the advisability and the value of empirical studies? That was four years ago. Something could have been done in this area over these years to provide some information on this subject.

JUSTICE REARDON: You are speaking of empirical studies on jury behavior?

MR. MacKENZIE: Yes, sir.

JUSTICE REARDON: The decision that was made very early on that, and it was a unanimous decision, by a meeting of some 25 men—if I gave you their names, I think you would recognize them—was that that study was difficult to mount and would not be helpful. It was almost an impossibility due to the nature which it necessarily must take.

I mentioned when I spoke here this evening the difficulties of assessing jury behavior. And any judge who has worked with jurors knows that. Sometimes a juror will lie, sometimes he will tell you the truth. Sometimes he is moved by things he doesn't recognize himself. He cannot sometimes assess what has happened to his subconscious and what he has heard. And anyone who has worked with large groups of jurors knows that to be so.

MR. MacKENZIE: There are techniques for trying to combat that problem, aren't there? They don't lie in the area of the judge's expertise, I appreciate, or line. But there are some ways of attempting that.

JUSTICE REARDON: Well, I don't know just what you mean by that.

MR. MacKENZIE: Well, some headshrinkers can figure out ways to find out if a person is lying actually, despite what he says.

JUDGE REARDON: I think we have enough head-shrinkers in the courts now, Mr. MacKenzie. [Laughter.]

MR. MacKENZIE: No. I'm really quite serious about this.

JUSTICE REARDON: No. I'm serious, too, in saying that the definite decision was made that an empirical study of jury behavior would not be of value because of the exceeding great difficulty to mount it and come up with anything meaningful. Now, there were one or two in that meeting who thought otherwise. There are still suggestions being made for empirical studies along that line. We are not adverse to them. But we questioned their feasibility. And that was very early in the game.

MR. FREEBURG: Judge Reardon, you made the statement at one point that you felt satisfied on this issue that the press had little public support.

JUSTICE REARDON: That's right.

MR. FREEBURG: Could you cite some examples for this prejudice?

JUSTICE REARDON: Yes.

MR. FREEBURG: —on your part?

JUSTICE REARDON: Yes.

MR. FREEBURG: Could you cite some examples as to why you feel this way?

JUSTICE REARDON: Yes. We have covered the United States press on clippings in a massive sense. We have picked up every letter that has been published in a newspaper of size around the country in the last three or four months. Certainly no one is writing, no one is complaining. The talk is between the local bar associations and the media, but nothing in the correspondence columns in the newspapers.

MR. FREEBURG: Why do you draw the conclusion that this means there is no public support for the press?

JUSTICE REARDON: Well, where would you expect it to be evinced? When the newspaper comes out with an editorial and says this report is arrogant and presumptive and so forth, wouldn't you expect a few people to write and say "Me too"? In the St. Louis *Globe-Democrat* I didn't see any letters.

A VOICE: You're right. There weren't.

JUSTICE REARDON: Yes.

MR. GARVER: Judge Reardon, I would like to go back to the question of prior criminal record. And I guess this is made in ignorance of the meaning of your report.

Is it your intention or the intention of this canon to preclude the press from resorting to the public record or their own files on a suspect's previous criminal record? Or does this apply only to what is disclosed in court?

JUSTICE REARDON: What we're saying is that the lawyers and the enforcement officials should not disclose prior criminal records to agents for publication. We don't feel we control this situation. I say "we" in the sense of the bench and the bar. If the newspaper in its own files has a story that Doaks is a member of the Mafia and has been in three or four times on this and that, the paper is free to print it.

MR. FREEBURG: But on that point what bothers me is a criminal record and not being able to print it. What if we have in our morgue some of these clippings that you talk about, but they are incomplete? They say that John Doe was arrested on such and such a date and he was charged with such and such a crime, but it ends there. We would like to go to the police department to check that record to see if he was freed in that case. Reporting that would be helping him. You're saying that we can print an incomplete record, and this is okay. But if we want to be accurate and go and check against the record at the police department, you are saying we can't do that, when it could help the man who has been arrested.

Secondly, and especially, in a political case where a man might have been arrested, what if these are in our morgue and we want to check to see if the records have been destroyed in some way? I think we have some rights here.

JUSTICE REARDON: I am sympathetic with eleemosynary inclinations of the *Tribune* in these matters. [Laughter.] But I stand on the recommendation. I think that you have in your morgue there a certain number of records. If you want to print them, you go ahead and print them. But we are saying to the district attorney of Cook county or the superintendent of the Chicago police, Orlando Wilson, or his successor, they can do what they want about it, but it isn't proper for you to release this stuff, not at this time.

MR. MacKENZIE: In talking about the public trial in the discussion section of the [ABA] Code, the discussion is that the right of a public trial is not a right of the public but rather a right of the accused. The same American Bar Association Minimum Standards Committee also issued and had approved on that same afternoon the report on a speedy trial, a right that stems from the same Sixth Amendment. In that report the ABA said the public interest in a speedy trial is so important that the granting of a dismissal of an indictment for want of a speedy trial will not turn on the threat to the defendant. Do you feel at all responsible for reconciling those two positions?

JUSTICE REARDON: No. As I view it, the Sixth Amendment guarantee of a speedy trial is tied in quite closely with the guarantee of a fair and impartial trial. The gentlemen who drafted the amendment I think equated them. There is an interrelationship between the right of a defendant to have his trial tried quickly, to have it tried in a venue which is satisfactory to him— the language of the amendment is "in the district where he is," I have forgotten the exact language—but close to home. And he can get that only if he can get a jury which comes, not impartial as it stands unsworn, but as nearly impartial as possible.

If in the district in which he lives he has a jury which has been presaturated by publicity on his activities, he loses his right to a speedy trial, he loses his right to a trial in his own district and he has been really kicked three ways in contravention of the amendment. Since the meeting in February I have managed to stay reasonably busy, and I have not read that report as completely as I should have, perhaps, to answer the question as well as I might. But that is the best thing I can tell you now.

MR. CONRAD: Judge, you have been asked a lot of large questions; I'll ask you a small one. It may seem like nitpicking but I think it represents some of the assumptions that the committee made. The recommendations preclude the release of the fact that a statement has been given by the accused.

JUSTICE REARDON: Yes.

MR. CONRAD: In addition to proscribing release of any details of the statement, just the fact that one has been given. What is prejudicial about public release of the fact that the accused has given a statement?

JUSTICE REARDON: This is debatable. I think the discussion which occurred on that point inside the committee was that if Captain Jones comes out and says "Well, Joe has given us a statement," the natural inference is that Joe hasn't given them a statement saying "It's not going to rain next Wednesday." We had some releases which did not indicate that Joe had confessed but that Joe had given a statement; but they were so framed that it was perfectly evident to anyone who read them that Joe had confessed. I think that is the basis of that particular prohibition or attempt to prohibit.

MR. PIERSON: Judge Reardon, of course you are acquainted with the recommendations of Judge Irving Kaufman's committee.

JUSTICE REARDON: Yes.

MR. PIERSON: This is a committee of the federal judiciary whose recommendations we at least read as substantially less restrictive than the recommendations of your committee. I am wondering whether the reason for the fewer restrictions upon the federal judiciary than upon the state judiciary shows generally a greater confidence in the federal judiciary than in the state. When you are dealing with the state jurisdictions, there is the problem of elected judges. They are almost always running for office. If this is true, won't it be better to reform those systems than to try to muzzle people from whom the press gets information? In other words, isn't there an alternative? If the manner of appointments and the caliber of judges were the same throughout the 50 state jurisdictions, the same as the federal judiciary, if Judge Kaufman's committee is right, that federal judges need less restriction, wouldn't this be a better way to approach it?

JUSTICE REARDON: First of all, I want to say that you have voiced a notion which to me is quaint in some respects.

MR. PIERSON: Quaint for Massachusetts.

JUSTICE REARDON: That all federal judges are better judges than state judges. I disagree with that right off the bat. And the second thing is that insofar as the

Kaufman recommendations are concerned, *The* [*New York*] *Times* came out with an editorial entitled Satisfactory Accommodation which stated in effect what you just said, Mr. Pierson, that they were somewhat less restrictive. They didn't touch contempt and they skirted preliminary hearings.

MR. PIERSON: Yes.

JUSTICE REARDON: But their situation is different, and Judge Kaufman was quick to point that out. After that editorial came out in *The Times*, he wrote a letter to *The Times* saying your editorial March 8th is refreshing in its candor and so forth, but recognize that the press, as well as the courts, has responsibility to insure that neither the public's right to be informed of the operation of its government nor the accused's right to a fair trial before an impartial jury is needlessly sacrificed.

Then he went on to say, in fairness to the American Bar Association's recommendations, I wish to point out that the report of the committee on the operation of the jury system of the Judicial Conference of the United States of which I am chairman, was directed at the free press-fair trial dilemma as manifested in the federal court. As we attempted to make clear in our report, the problem in a state court context to which the Reardon Report also addressed itself was of a somewhat different nature.

Now, that is true. There was no need for them, for instance, to go into the law enforcement side of it. The [Justice] Department has regulations in being which are almost identical with ours. So if you add the change in the canon, which they bought, if you take the Sheppard case, the venue continuance provisions and the rest and you take the Department of Justice guideline, you have got about everything we had to say with the exception of contempt.

MR. PIERSON: Without revealing any confidences, I appeared before Judge Kaufman's committee, and I gather that they felt that their problem was much less in the federal judiciary than in the state, and primarily because the jurisdiction could have elected judges. But it seems to me that if you get any lesson out of the Sheppard case, it is primarily that both the prosecuting attorney and the judge were then running for election.

JUSTICE REARDON: That is true.

MR. PIERSON: I don't see how you can overlook that problem in the state courts and not at least do something to cure it as a Bar Association.

JUSTICE REARDON: Of course there have been some critiques of the Sheppard case that belabored Judge Blythin who has shuffled off this mortal coil and completely forgot Mr. Louis Seltzer, who had something to do with all the original publicity. The emphasis of the Sheppard case was on the trial judge, but a great deal of what went on there had taken place long before the case ever reached him.

MR. PIERSON: But what did your report do about Louis Seltzer, who was a crusader utterly dedicated to the idea that the local establishment was trying to defend a murderer? Nothing that he said in advance of the trial would have been stopped by any of your proposals.

JUSTICE REARDON: I'm not so certain about that. It seems to me that some of the material which he employed he had procured somewhat—

MR. PIERSON: He had banner headlines challenging the law enforcement agencies—

JUSTICE REARDON: Yes.

MR. PIERSON: —and it certainly wasn't from information he got from them. You are not suggesting that your report would have prevented him from that crusade, are you?

JUSTICE REARDON: No. No.

MR. PIERSON: So Louis Setlzer could do the same thing today if he were so disposed.

JUSTICE REARDON: Providing that—with the possible exception of—

MR. PIERSON: Except during the trial.

JUSTICE REARDON: And excepting the information that he received from official sources. I'm not certain about that.

MR. PIERSON: Well, the great complaint was that he wasn't getting information, or was getting misinformation from them.

JUSTICE REARDON: Yes. Well, that one is in the books. There will be more.

SECOND SESSION

WALTER GARVER, U. S. Chamber of Commerce: Mr. Daniel, some of the press, for competitive reasons, I suppose, in competition for readership, have, I think, and I ask you if this is not true, created much of this problem by what I would call the—little more than the "trial in the press," or on the printed page which results characterizing the suspect or accused person beyond the point where what happens in terms of legal and official justice is so much at odds with the image created in that kind of press, that the judicial process is cast into disfavor as a result of the difference between the judicial determination and the popular idea of just what kind of a person the accused was and whether it is believable that he really didn't do it.

And I think it is this kind of frictional competition on the part of the public press which has created much of this problem with regard to freedom, because people are extremely reluctant to disbelieve what they have seen in print.

So I ask you, isn't it an important part of the problem

that we as just ordinary citizens with some sense of responsibility for ongoing justice have come to feel that in the judicial process the results so often hinge on mere legal technicalities or complexities, or at least seem to, with the result that people are apt to feel dubious of justice because of the impressions they get from the sensational press stories.

MR. DANIEL: Mr. Garver, it seems to me that your question divides itself into three parts.

First of all, let's take the suggestion that newspapers in their desire for circulation or readership do certain things. The fact of the matter is that crime doesn't pay for the press like it used to. I am not talking now only about *The New York Times,* which is a rather more serious newspaper than some. We don't sell newspapers very much any more on crime. We sell it on all kinds of things. We will sell a good deal more newspapers on the assassination of Dr. Martin Luther King than we will on a sensational murder case. Now, admittedly, both are crimes. But we aren't talking about the same order of things here, the same type of crime.

We sell a lot of newspapers on the death of Dr. King not because he was murdered, but because he was Dr. King. In fact, as a matter of information to some of you, the largest daily circulation in the history of *The New York Times*—and Luther Huston who used to work with us will appreciate this—the largest circulation we ever achieved was with that issue reporting Dr. King was shot. This applies to all newspapers. As I tried to indicate in my prepared remarks, newspapers are not as sensational as they used to be.

Newspapers aren't sold any more on the street corner by a kid yelling out the headlines. They are tossed onto the front porch or into the bushes by a boy on a bicycle. And they are not sold on headlines at all. You don't see the headlines. The paper is all wrapped up and a rubber band is put around it. You buy the paper as a part of your daily ration of news and information. Newspapers, and television and radio as well, are changing in that sense. They are becoming more serious, more responsible.

Secondly, it seems to me you are confusing two things. One, you are saying it is a bad thing for people to blacken the reputations of people. What you said was "to blacken the reputation of somebody just to sell papers." You are absolutely right about that. We have no right, no justification for simply blackening people's reputations in order to create a sensation and sell newspapers. I would agree with that immediately.

But interference with the judicial process is a separate matter, in my mind. We have no right, it seems to me, unduly to prejudice the atmosphere, as perhaps was done in the case of Dr. Sheppard, for our own commercial ends. But we must be very careful when we say that, and when we try to place restrictions on that, so that we don't destroy the effectiveness of the press in one of its most important functions, which is to exercise a constant surveillance over the governmental system as a whole, the judicial process, the police, and so forth, to see that justice is being done. That is one of our functions.

Now, you can complain that people's reputations are blackened. Nobody ever seems to mention all the innocent people for whom the press speaks up. You can cite case after case after case of police brutality or third-degree methods or extorted confessions—not so much any more since the Supreme Court has made these things beyond the pale. But it used to be quite true. Prison brutality and corruption of judges and prosecutors and so forth, these things have been exposed by the newspapers. Let's not forget those things. I think we must all agree that blackening the reputation of people just casually and capriciously and for commercial gain is wrong. But let us remember that it isn't always blackening reputations that the press does. Sometimes it is saving reputations. We have done it in the newspaper I work on; and newspapers of the more crusading type have done it far more often than we have. The press is a protection for the citizen as well as, sometimes, a burden for him to bear.

ROBERT WILLSON, The George Washington University: Mr. Daniel, in your opening remarks you referred to the American Newspaper Publishers Association study to determine whether pre-trial publicity really seriously prejudices a fair trial. Would you distinguish for me, please, between serious prejudice of a trial and just plain ordinary everyday prejudice of a fair trial?

MR. DANIEL: Maybe I chose my adverbs wrongly.

But let me say a word about that study. I don't want to give any undue support or publicity here to Justice Reardon, but Justice Reardon will argue, if he hasn't already done so in this room, that this study was not necessary; that the American Bar Association and its committee, his committee, already knew everything it needed to know about this matter; and that, in any case, the study wasn't going to be of any value because it was not going to be a study of jurors and their reactions but a series of interviews with trial judges and a study of the literature. You might question the terms of reference of the study, as he did.

But if Justice Reardon and others don't like the study or don't like the terms of reference, why don't they conduct one themselves? The fact of the matter is that no such study has ever been conducted by anybody.

One of the very prominent members of Justice Reardon's committee, Judge Bernard S. Meyer, a very distinguished and serious judge of the New York Supreme Court in Nassau County, will tell you that there is no empirical data at all on this subject. Nobody really knows whether—and if you will quote my words back to me, I will repeat them—nobody knows really whether pre-trial publicity seriously affects the minds of jurors.

Obviously, the minds of jurors are affected by all kinds of things. If you are going to try to get a system that will strain out every single little teeny-weeny bit of prejudice that could possibly seep into the mind of a juror, you are going to have what you have now, unfortunately. It takes three and four weeks sometimes to select a jury. It is the most ridiculous system, I think, that exists on the face of the globe for setting up a trial.

I rather guess that maybe you are a law professor—I hope so anyway—because if you are, you will know better than I do that they don't do this in other countries, where justice, I might say, is done just as well as it is here. England, for example. They don't spend three and four weeks choosing a jury. The judge takes over the questioning and in about one hour he seats the jury; two hours later, the trial is over.

If we had justice done as expeditiously in this country, we really wouldn't be arguing here about anything. Maters would go much better for us all.

MARJORIE GIRTH, Brookings Institution: It seems to me from Justice Reardon's statement that he wasn't trying to screen out everything that might possibly affect a juror. What he was trying to screen out was information about prior criminal records and existence, if any, of a confession. Now, that is not really everything that might possibly affect a juror.

MR. DANIEL: I think you are right about Justice Reardon. It just doesn't happen that I agree with him. I think your interpretation of his remarks is probably quite correct.

Let's take prior criminal records. I remarked that I had sat on the platform of the American Society of Newspaper Editors here some years ago with Judge Skelly Wright and some others. At that time Mr. Katzenbach, who was then the attorney general, spoke. He made the point that the Department of Justice would make no effort to conceal the prior criminal records of defendants if anybody wanted them. They were public records. If you wanted to come and ask for them, the Department of Justice would give them to you. He had no intention of trying to suppress them. I think that is probably still the rule at the Department of Justice.

Most newspapermen, most radio and television broadcasters, agree with me that this business of indiscriminately putting confessions, or so-called confessions, into the paper and quoting from them and offering them to the public as the gospel is wrong. But remember what I said a moment ago about some of the good things we do. News media have for a long, long time been against beating prisoners in the back room and extorting confessions from them. The fact that we mention a confession in the paper doesn't necessarily mean that we think it is true. It might mean that it is so ridiculous that the public ought to know about it. And if we can, we should discover how it was obtained.

This is where the problem lies. It is not with printing the mere statement in the paper that a confession was obtained. What is crucial is how it was obtained and how valid it is. That is what the legal profession should apply its mind to, in my opinion, and that is what serious judges do apply themselves to.

I agree that confessions at times should not be used and should be closely qualified. If you say that a statement was obtained from a defendant, that is really about as far as you should go. You certainly shouldn't quote from it or characterize it, unless you know it has been properly passed on by the authorities and you know it is reliable and admissible as evidence.

But let's take the matter of prior criminal records. What some lawyers are asking us to do, Justice Reardon among them, is really ridiculous. Let's take the case of Frank Costello, a very well known—I say this now, you see; this is the kind of thing I am not supposed to say in the newspaper—a well-known member of the Mafia rackets. I'm not supposed to say that in the newspaper, because that will prejudice the poor man's chances if he goes into court.

I can say that Costello is a family man; he has four children; he has a nice home in Sands Point; he provides well for his family; and he goes to mass every Sunday (I don't know whether he does or not). I can say all that sort of thing about him. But if I say that he is a notorious racketeer and has a police record as long as my arm, that is prejudicial. Of course it is ridiculous, this kind of thing. Prejudices can run both ways, you know.

Let's take another case: A kid whose career in crime is only just beginning. He has made a mis-step and he has a little bit of a record. Then he is accused of a very serious crime. I think it is highly prejudicial, if he is accused of murder, to say that he also stole bananas off the fruit stand when he was 16 years old. There I agree with you that criminal records are prejudicial and shouldn't be printed. But to go to the ridiculous lengths of saying that well-known criminals shouldn't be described in the newspapers as well-known criminals is just fantastic.

You know all that Mafia gang that met up at Apalachin, New York (I think that's the way they pronounce it. It's Appalachian where I came from). After that meeting we were called up by the judge and asked, please, not to mention the prior criminal records of all these charming gentlemen who were attending a barbecue there because it might result in a mistrial and these fellows would get off. This is the most ridiculous thing I have ever heard of. I hasten to add that we complied with the judge's request because we didn't want to bear the responsibility for a mistrial.

There was another meeting in Queens. We write about a bunch of fellows who are arrested in a restaurant in Queens. What is the charge against them? The charge against them is consorting with known criminals. Who are the known criminals? Each other. [Laughter.] And we're not supposed to say that these fellows have criminal records. These things just get to the point of being ridiculous.

What we need in all of this in my view is a little common sense, and not these pontifical declarations on the part of the ABA, Justice Reardon's committee, that under no circumstances at any time should you ever mention anybody's prior criminal record. This is just nonsense.

LUTHER HUSTON, *Editor and Publisher:* Luther Huston, *Editor and Publisher* and erstwhile *New York Times.*

Mr. Daniel, since the assassination of Dr. King the FBI and the Justice Department have been giving out a good deal of information about this James Earl Ray who is supposed to have been the assassin. They have said a lot about his past record, that he is a convict and all that. The papers have printed that, and in so doing, don't you agree that the newspapers there are aiding the cause of justice by giving information to the public that may help the FBI to catch this fellow? And if the restrictions of the Reardon Report were put on, wouldn't it be impossible for the newspapers in that way to give assistance to the cause of justice?

MR. DANIEL: Well, sir, you asked me if I don't agree with you. I couldn't stand up here and disagree with you on anything. [Laughter.] So you put me in an embarrassing position. But as it so happens, I do agree with you. I think that in fairness we should say that the Reardon Report and the people who support it do make an exception in cases where the release of information is thought to be needed in order to apprehend a fugitive. And that is done in this case.

Of course some day somebody will, I suppose, end up by saying the poor man will never be able to get a fair trial because by the time he is found, if he ever is found, the public will be so convinced that he was indeed the murderer that you can't find a jury in the whole United

States that will be able to try him fairly. That, incidentally, is again, as you will have heard me say, where I depart from the Reardon committee and other people who argue the same way.

I think, myself, that I could give this man a fair trial. I think you could. I think any of you people here could. I am not convinced that just because Ray is a former convict and had some unpleasant traits and habits, that I would be unable to give him a fair trial. I am not at all convinced that just because he is an ex-convict that he shot Dr. King. I want some evidence of that. And so far I have had none. Absolutely none.

I have had evidence that somebody shot Dr. King, that there was a gun, there was a suitcase, there was a man who fled, there was a car that went around the corner and was later abandoned. I have a lot of things, but none of them add up to the assassination of Dr. King; not by this man, anyway. Somebody shot him, obviously.

I don't hold with this business that informed, intelligent citizens can't clear their minds sufficiently of prejudice to give a fair trial to a man who is obviously an unfortunate man, perhaps an underprivileged man, a man who has perhaps a history of some mental disturbance. Goodness only knows what this man's problems are. I think we could give him a fair trial, any of us.

PAUL CONRAD, National Newspaper Association: Mr. Daniel, you suggested that there is a trend within the press for its self-restraint and the use of maturity and more responsibility. We are all here looking for a solution to this overall problem. Perhaps there is a general feeling that if sufficient restraint could be employed by the news media that this maybe would be a solution. But I suspect that there are many who doubt that there are enough editors who have the kind of conscience that you suggested when you mentioned soul-searching.

Haven't you suggested another very important area when you described the case where the judge asked you to withhold certain information because of potential mistrial? Isn't this another area which you haven't dwelled upon and which hasn't been mentioned to any great extent in all this debate on free press and fair trial. There is the built-in restraint that comes now as the press is very conscious of the fact that, if it exposes certain types of information, confessions, certain probative information, in advance of the trial, it is very possible there will be a mistrial or there will be a change of venue. There is the apprehension that this will be assigned directly in the public mind to the news media that released that information.

MR. DANIEL: I think it is certainly true, Mr. Conrad, that this is happening. If I may say so, I think that the legal profession and the judges are trying to put the onus on the press for this entirely too much. As one eminent justice of the Supreme Court remarked to me after the Sheppard case, judges are going far beyond what was intended in the Sheppard case. They are leaping way out ahead of that. They are going too far and too fast, faster than the Supreme Court ever intended them to.

Judges like to have good records, I suppose, and they don't want to be reversed on appeal. So the safest way, if there is any chance of being reversed, is to declare a mistrial and start all over again.

To my way of thinking, that isn't necessarily the most responsible way to approach matters. Let me cite another case in New York. I'm sorry I can't remember the name of the man, but again he was one of those Mafia fellows and a very well known one. *The New York Times* and the *New York Daily News* and, I believe, *Newsday*, when he was brought to trial in New York some months ago, mentioned in one form or another that he had a police record or that he was thought by the FBI to be a member of the Mafia or had been listed by the FBI as a Mafia chief, or something of that sort. The judge, who was a supreme court judge in New York, promptly declared a mistrial and ordered a change of venue. He took the case up to Albany. When he got up there he warned everybody not to print this stuff in the papers and nobody did. And the trial went off and the fellow was convicted.

Now, the thing about this is that the judge in this case, we felt, had been looking for an opportunity to declare a mistrial. He had threatened to do it three or four times. He had a terrible urge to do it, so he finally found himself a case and he did. But he didn't do the defendant any favor. He may have done himself a favor, but he didn't do the defendant any favor.

So far as I could gather, the defendant's lawyers were appalled. They were going to have to go up to Albany with a bunch of rural hicks who didn't like Italians from New York anyway. You know, these fellows all talk out of the corner of their mouth and so forth and these fellows, these country juries up in Albany—I say "country." I come from the country myself; I feel free to speak about it. The defendant's lawyers didn't want this trial in Albany; that's the last place they wanted to go. They wanted to be tried down in New York where people of their own kind could understand them and know what kind of people they were. They lost the case and, of course, the defendant won't be in jail for the next four or five years. This is another thing wrong with justice.

JOHN MacKENZIE, *Washington Post:* You speak so seriously about the study that I am prompted to ask you whether the study was not an instrument of delay chiefly and very little else. It seems that whenever you want to delay something you call for a study of the situation.

MR. DANIEL: You are talking now about the ANPA study?

MR. MacKENZIE: Yes, it was offered as the reason why the ABA should postpone its vote.

MR. DANIEL: You're a brave man here to stand up

and criticize publishers in this meeting—[laughter]—but—

MR. MacKENZIE: I only put it as a question. [Laughter.]

MR. DANIEL: You might be right, Mr. MacKenzie. I'm not any more scared of publishers than you are. Let me put it another way. The ANPA perhaps didn't come forward with this until it saw that it didn't have any other recourse. I agree with that.

If it had really wanted such a study, it should have come forward with it a long time ago. But that still doesn't absolve us in the profession, or the legal profession, from giving serious consideration to this matter. Justice Reardon just brushes it all aside and says, "Oh, we know." I don't happen to have his quotations in front of me but Justice Reardon says, "Oh, we know all this. There's nothing that we can learn. We've been through it all."

I'm not convinced of that. I've tried to cite cases, and I've cited only a few by way of illustration, to demonstrate that it's not all that clear cut that what you say in the newspapers necessarily influences jurors. It's rather a despairing thought to think how little attention is paid to the newspapers sometimes. But you, working on the *Washington Post*, you know better than I do, or as well as I do certainly, how much serious thought we give to these matters these days. We are not out to pander to the worst tastes of the public just to sell a few newspapers. That's not the way we run newspapers these days. That's not even the way they run newspapers in Keokuk, much less in big towns like Washington and New York.

MR. MacKENZIE: I would like to say to you that I'm one who wishes that a study were made because we just don't know enough about juries anyhow. I was sorry that the ABA didn't make it and I'm a little bit sorry that the publishers won't follow through with a study like that. I think the proof of that—this should be a question—but the proof of it is that it is not going through, as far as I have heard.

MR. DANIEL: I think the ANPA intends to go ahead with it, so far as I know. I hope they do. But, if they do, I would recommend that they change the terms of reference and make it a really serious sociological study rather than allow what I think is going to be a rather superficial job. In that sense they lay themselves open to criticisms from Justice Reardon, it seems to me.

BARRY SCHWEID, Associated Press: You seem to be concerned about secrecy. Can you tell me why then you find voluntary codes all right? Is it just that it's self-imposed rather than imposed by the outside? How is that any less secret?

MR. DANIEL: I didn't know that I had betrayed any unusual concern about secrecy, but we could have—

MR. SCHWEID: You said of the Soviet Union— [Mr. Schweid and Mr. Daniel both talking.]

MR. DANIEL: I think that question almost answers itself. I would be appalled, as I am sure you would be, if we had a system in this country where you simply didn't know what was going on behind those courtroom doors. Now I know the ABA is not proposing to close all courtroom doors in this country. I am a little bit frightened on behalf of the newspapers, first of all, but on behalf of the public, most of all, by any notion of introducing a greater element of secrecy into the legal process here.

In that case, why voluntary codes? No voluntary code that I know of undertakes to promise that newspapermen will stay out of the courtroom voluntarily. I agree entirely with the point which I think you are making here, that a voluntary code is quite a different matter from an imposed code. To impose a code on the press, you have to do one of two things. You have to establish a censorship in some form; I don't care what you call it, it's a censorship. Or you have to impose licensing. Otherwise you have no sanctions against the press at all. And the moment you do either one of these things in even the slightest degree you no longer have freedom of the press. Freedom is freedom, you know. It isn't freedom by permission of the American Bar Association. Freedom is freedom and that's it.

MR. SCHWEID: Yes, but I thought you were talking too about the freedom of the public to know. I don't know how that freedom is preserved if the press in cooperation with the authorities voluntarily censors and doesn't tell the public. In other words, if the press is the judge of the public's right to know and the public isn't told, I don't know why that's a preferable situation to the Bar Association deciding what the public shouldn't be told.

MR. DANIEL: I haven't ever seen it suggested by anybody in the press that the right to know shall be more than temporarily withheld. It's a matter of timing rather than anything else. No code has said, "We hereby swear that we will never ever tell such and such things that happen in court." We will tell at the proper time. That's one aspect of it.

The other thing is that it is the press now that decides what the public ought to know. We decide every day. You do, he does, he does (pointing to newspaperman). We all decide what the public ought to know. But the essence of freedom of the press is that if some fellow doesn't like what we decide he can go out and tell it on the street corner, or he can call a meeting and complain, or he can establish a newspaper and print it himself. This is what the essence of freedom of the press is, in my view.

MR. SCHWEID: Yes, and yet if a man has a Mafia connection and the judge asks the newspaper, "Don't publish it," then somehow you are not telling the public about the man's connection with the Mafia. I'm having difficulty understanding why that's an admirable position to take.

MR. DANIEL: I don't think it's admirable. I have seen newspapers do it and I have been on a newspaper that did it. What I'm arguing, I hope I haven't been misunderstood, is that withholding anything so obvious as that Mafia connection is ridiculous. Let me go back to what I said. If it's a boy who is in trouble for the first time, or somebody who doesn't have a long criminal record, somebody who is not known in the community as a thug or a thief or a racketeer, I think it's perhaps fair to give him a break. Perhaps it's fair not to tell about his previous criminal record until he has had a proper trial before a jury. Then tell it all. That's all I've suggested.

Let me give you an example. Let's not take the Mafia for a moment. Let me give an example that occurred in Dallas. I don't remember the name of the case and it's not important. It was told to me by Felix McKnight, who is the editor of the *Dallas Times-Herald*. They had a case down there where a young man ran down and killed a pedestrian on the street. This young man had had 30 convictions for traffic violations. The newspaper printed that fact, and there was a great outcry that this was prejudicial to this fellow.

The outcry, to my way of thinking, should have been against the authorities who allowed the man with 30 convictions to continue to drive an automobile in the streets of Dallas and menace the lives of the citizens. What the hell do the citizens want? Do they want their lives protected or do they want the right of this kind of a man to drive an automobile protected?

THEODORE PIERSON, lawyer representing Radio, Television News Directors Association: I am a member of the profession that you have spent a major portion of your time putting down. I am a lawyer and I am somewhat indignant about some of your comments, but that indignation is restrained by the fact that I also have professional commitments as you do.

You have suggested that the lawyers ought to put their own house in order. But you also spoke of the conscience of the press. In this last exchange you have been speaking of codes. You also referred to your calling as a profession. It is my understanding that one of the elements of a profession is the adoption of voluntary codes of ethics. It is also my understanding that no major newspaper or press association has ever been able to agree upon a code inaugurated by its profession by which it would live. But the only code you are talking about is one like *The Washington Post,* or *The New York Times* adopts for itself. But the professionals in your business refuse to be found by a common code applicable to their profession.

Now, I think H. L. Mencken some years ago referred to press codes as so much "moonshine" and the reason he gave was that the members of the press are basically "swine."

MR. DANIEL: Are basically what? [Laughter.]

MR. PIERSON: Swine. Do you think that has changed or not? [Laughter.]

MR. DANIEL: Let me answer the question about the latter remark.

MR. PIERSON: It's Mencken's not mine. [Laughter.]

MR. DANIEL: I understand. He lived in another

day. He probably wouldn't approve of this fact, but on *The New York Times* the principal writers on legal subjects both happen to be lawyers. If they don't know the law and how to handle it, or if they are of low character, I'm afraid we'll have to attribute that to a profession that does have a code of ethics.

MR. PIERSON: You get back to us. [Laughter.]

MR. DANIEL: Yes. In Mencken's day it may have been true that people in our profession were of a rather low order. But we're doing our best, as I trust you are doing in the legal profession, to raise the level of competence of our people in this area as in all others.

I said I wasn't going to rebut Justice Reardon and I don't intend to do so, but I would mention that Justice Reardon suggested we should have people writing about the law of the same competence who write about education and the sciences and so forth. We do.

MR. PIERSON: *The New York Times* does.

MR. DANIEL: We do, not only *The New York Times* but *The Washington Post.*

Many other newspapers, the *Louisville Courier-Journal.* I don't happen to have a list of them but I'm going to get one if I stay in this business.

About the code of ethics: You talk and many of our critics talk as if the only law that the press knows is the law of the jungle. There is a very well-defined code of ethics in our profession and, if I may say so, we observe it with as much fidelity as the legal profession observes its code.

MR. PIERSON: That's nothing to boast about.

MR. DANIEL: I know it isn't. [Laughter.] That's why I mention it. And it isn't written down by an association. We don't have a professional association that controls its members. We don't intend to have one. I don't see how the press can remain free if you set up a czar to run it or if you set up an association to decide what it shall do.

I am not opposed, incidentally, to the kind of thing they have in England, a press council which passes judgment on the behavior of the press and issues strictures against bad behavior by the press. But I would be very much opposed to any sort of licensing of the press or licensing of newspapermen.

As to the vaunted professional standards of the legal profession, you don't have to take criticism from me. Just turn to what Justice Clark has been saying lately. He is, I believe now, heading an institute that is going to try to remedy some of these things. See what he has been saying about the appalling situation in the legal profession when it comes to enforcing discipline on its members, the tiny number of cases.

MR. PIERSON: What about the other side of that picture?

MR. DANIEL: I understand. I grew up in the Associated Press, which has a very strict and a very distinct code of ethics. It's basic, and it's standard for the whole profession, really. We all base our own performance on it.

We don't have any board to enforce it. We don't bar people from practicing the profession of journalism. I'll call it a trade, if you like it better. But we do maintain, I think, a very high standard of conduct and, if you don't think so, try bribing a newspaperman sometime. [Laughter.]

MR. PIERSON: I'd need a lawyer, I think.

MR. DANIEL: Sir?

MR. PIERSON: I think I'd need a lawyer, if I did.

MR. DANIEL: I hope you'd need one, because I think the standard is very high. And what we have been talking about in this matter, I trust, is raising that standard further. It has been raised, within this period that we are talking about, since the Warren Commission Report. I think the standards of the profession in regard to reporting crime news have been raised. I tried to say that. I will repeat it again.

I think our standards are going to be raised further, but I believe it's going to be accomplished by voluntary codes adopted by the newspapers themselves in collaboration with the bar. I sincerely hope it doesn't come down to the matter of letting the lawyers or the judges or the legislators establish their code for the newspapers and then in some way trying to enforce it. I don't think they'll succeed, first of all.

MR. PIERSON: I must say I agree with you on your last statement.

MR. DANIEL: We had better be careful or you and I are going to agree before we—

MR. PIERSON: I've been trying to avoid that. [Laughter.] But I don't quite understand your statement that you would favor a voluntary press-bar code. If it were meaningful it would be binding upon the press—

MR. DANIEL: The standards are not binding.

MR. PIERSON: Then what's the use of having them?

MR. DANIEL: What's the use of having standards in any respect?

MR. PIERSON: I don't know.

MR. DANIEL: What's the use of belonging to a church, let's say, where there are certain standards of behavior set up and people try to conform to them in their lives? What's the point of belonging to a religious group? For that matter, what is the point of belonging to a bar association?

MR. PIERSON: I don't know.

MR. DANIEL: There are certain standards there. You all don't abide by them but God knows how bad it would be if you didn't have the standards.

MR. PIERSON: Yes, but you are highly critical because we didn't. It seems to me your organization is saying that we don't abide by codes because we aren't willing to be bound by them.

I don't know whether it would be better to have something that you can publish and say we are highly professional, we are oriented to the interest and needs of the community, we are concerned about the defendant. But this is just a price of paper that you sit down with the bar and write up. You say the standards are not binding, and it seems to me you said they ought not to be binding, the press ought to be free.

MR. DANIEL: I have said very plainly that I have no objection to whatever the bar wishes to do about disciplining its own members. But what I do object to is when the bar starts disciplining me.

MR. PIERSON: Well, on that you and I agree. We're not talking about the bar doing this.

MR. DANIEL: Judge Reardon is talking about that.

MR. PIERSON: Yes. Well, I am not in complete agreement with him, as most of us here know.

But you were talking about the conscience of the newspaper, fulfilling responsibility. And yet you, it seems to me, say that no code, whether joint, with press and bar, or within the press itself, has any real efficacy beyond what each individual newspaper or press association decides at a given moment to—

MR. DANIEL: When did I say that?

MR. PIERSON: If you didn't say that, then I misunderstood you.

MR. DANIEL: Well, you certainly did. I haven't said anything like that that I am aware of. We have it all recorded. We can find out.

MR. PIERSON: Well, are you in favor of press-bar codes?

MR. DANIEL: I said very clearly that the press and the bar were collaborating, a number of codes had been adopted, and more were going to be adopted. I expressed no disagreement with or disapproval of them.

MR. PIERSON: But you say they are not binding.

MR. DANIEL: But they are not binding. None of them are binding. Absolutely none of them is binding. I don't want them to be binding. But that doesn't mean that they have no efficacy.

MR. PIERSON: Well, what is their efficacy?

MR. DANIEL: The efficacy, if I am not boring you by repeating myself, is the same as that inherent in a moral standard that you set up in a religious group. Nobody is bound to obey the Ten Commandments, except insofar as he may violate the law in doing so and may be arrested for it.

MR. PIERSON: Most violations of the Ten Commandments are violations of the law.

MR. DANIEL: Well, I said except insofar as he may violate the law. Don't misquote me again. But nobody is required to love his neighbor. The fact that he is enjoined to do so is certainly not a bad thing. But you would have it that we shouldn't even say that unless we are going to *make* him love his neighbor.

MR. PIERSON: I think I understand. You are in favor of prior statements so long as they are not binding.

MR. DANIEL: I am in favor of codes of ethics, as long as they do not involve censorship or licensing of the press. That is as briefly as I can say it.

RUSSELL FREEBURG, *Chicago Tribune:* I am reminded of a story about David Kennedy last week, when he was involved in a rock-throwing incident here.

The claim was made that by the use of his name the juvenile court code had been broken and so on. *The (Washington) Post* took the attitude, and we did also, that since his father (Senator Robert Kennedy) had issued a statement it was all right to use his name, to go ahead with the story. I don't recall if *The New York Times* printed the story. Did you? Are you familiar with the story and did you print it?

MR. DANIEL: I don't happen to remember whether we printed it or not. But I think we certainly should have, if we didn't. I believe we did.

This is a common question. It doesn't so much involve fair trial—

MR. FREEBURG: No.

MR. DANIEL: —because the boy is not on trial, and probably never will be.

But we have this question arise frequently when kids are arrested. In general our policy, and I think the policy of most newspapers, is not to use the name when we are asked not to use it. Or, when it is against the accepted procedures or the rules of the court—I don't remember what it happens to be in New York state—we don't use it.

But when it happens to be the son of a prominent father and it is common knowledge in the community, I am afraid we do use it. There is no point in not using it. We are not concealing anything, we are not protecting anybody. And, as you say, in this case the boy's father issued a statement, for the obvious reason, I should imagine, that he knew that it was known. I thought it was a very nice statement, incidentally. He said what any sensible father would say about his child: He was a little bit wayward, certainly not a bad boy, I believe he said.

MR. FREEBURG: He was a good boy.

MR. DANIEL: He is a good boy. Yes. He is a good boy.

MR. MacKENZIE: I am not a fan of the Reardon Report, but your statement troubles me about the Mafia man who goes on trial. You say it is ridiculous not to report that he is listed by the FBI as a member of the Mafia. That really disturbs me. Do you think that a jury can be impartial if it is exposed to that statement?

MR. DANIEL: Well, yes, a juror can be impartial if exposed to that statement. I don't know why you think he couldn't. I don't understand this reasoning that simply because you have been told an alleged fact about a man that you therefore immediately form an opinion of his guilt in a particular incident. This is the kind of lack of confidence in the jury system that perturbs me as much as the statement perturbs you.

I again repeat, it is only the notorious criminal that I'm talking about where you put this in—so notorious that everybody knows who he is anyway. What is the point of concealing from the public, which already knows, the fact that he is a notorious criminal? I don't get the point of that.

MR. MacKENZIE: I really can't name more than a dozen notorious criminals.

MR. DANIEL: Well, you see, you don't read the newspapers carefully. [Laughter.]

MR. MacKENZIE: No. I guess not. [Laughter.]

MR. DANIEL: Because we print stories about them all the time.

I don't happen to be able to knock them off on my fingers. But—Luchese, Gambino, you know, all these fellows.

MR. MacKENZIE: Yes.

MR. DANIEL: Their names are all familiar to me. They must be familiar to you.

MR. MacKENZIE: I don't know the name—

MR. DANIEL: In other days you have heard of John Dillinger, and you have heard of—

MR. MacKENZIE: I don't know the name of Gambino's brother.

MR. DANIEL: You don't know the name of his brother?

MR. MacKENZIE: Yes. Except that it is Gambino.

MR. DANIEL: Yes. But you know his name is Gambino.

MR. MacKENZIE: Yes.

MR. DANIEL: But you have a little bit of suspicion that maybe he is related to the other Gambino.

MR. MacKENZIE: Yes. I submit that making that kind of judgment as to what to print, especially where it may go to trial, is going to bring the system down.

MR. DANIEL: Oh, my goodness. "Bring the system down." What do you mean by bringing the system down? I was sitting today with a lawyer. He happened to be my own lawyer. I was in North Carolina. I was asking him about the new court reform they have instituted down there and what it meant. It is a new system of courts. He told me about it. I said I hoped this would work out well, it sounded like a good system. And he said, "Yes, if it works out, it might be that before long we will be able to get a case to trial in less than a year."

That is what is wrong with the courts. This business of worrying about whether Gambino's criminal record is mentioned in the newspapers when everybody in town knows his reputation is not what is wrong with the system. What is wrong with the system is that you can't get Gambino to trial and you can't get him convicted and you can't get him in jail because lawyers are using every single obstructive device they possibly can to keep the fellow out of jail.

We have a case in New York right now that is being tried, a hijacking case involving some of these very fellows whose names you don't happen to know, whose criminal records—[laughter]—you have never heard of. The hijacking case took place in 1959! And they are probably going to be convicted this week. This is the one where Valachi was called into the case.

There will then be three or four more years before there is a final determination. Where is justice in this kind of case?

MR. MacKENZIE: The solution is not to talk about their criminal record.

MR. DANIEL: Well, the solution is to get on with cases and try them so we don't have this business of suppressing news for years and years and years and years, which is what Justice Reardon wants you to do. He doesn't want you to mention this man's criminal record and activities for nine years. You have to wait for ten years or 15 years until the case is disposed of.

You don't have any opportunity to say in the paper: "There is a thief, a racketeer, going around this town loose because the judges won't put him in jail." You can't mention it. Justice Reardon would have you not say a word about it.

MR. MacKENZIE: He doesn't say that.

MR. DANIEL: Yes, he does.

MR. MacKENZIE: He doesn't say the press shouldn't print that.

MR. DANIEL: Yes, he does.

MR. MacKENZIE: That's not what he says. What he says is that the public official shouldn't contribute to that by divulging information. He doesn't say that the press shouldn't print that.

MR. DANIEL: And if the judge issues an order that the press shouldn't say that and the press says it, Justice Reardon would have some newsman put in jail for contempt of court.

MR. SCHWEID: Along the same lines I would be interested in your comments about phrases that I see in newspapers that go something to the effect: "reputed king of the so-and-so underworld." If a man has possibly an income tax evasion conviction standing against him, do you think newspapers are justified in ordaining some of these people kings of anything?

MR. DANIEL: Well, suppose you in your profession were writing a story about Al Capone.

MR. SCHWEID: We have live people who are very much like that.

MR. DANIEL: What would you call him? What would you call him?

MR. SCHWEID: Well, I have that problem. We have a fellow, Paul DeLucia, Paul Ricca, of Chicago. Apparently all they have on him in this country is some income tax evasion. The authorities are trying to send him to Italy, where he doesn't want to go. It's something —I'm being quite frank—I don't know quite how to handle. I don't quite know how to—

MR. DANIEL: There is no problem about handling it.

MR. SCHWEID:—refer to him.

MR. DANIEL: There is no problem about handling it if the man is notorious. But there is a problem about handling it if he is not notorious. There is a problem, as someone said here, about handling it if it is too near the trial or if it is likely to inflame the passions of the lethargic jury.

MR. SCHWEID: Well, you are not suggesting the word "notorious" here.

MR. DANIEL: There are problems here. But you don't give me a very good one. As I say, let's take Al Capone. What do you call him? A businessman? A

Chicago businessman? "Chicago Businessman Held on Income Tax Evasion."

MR. SCHWEID: I quite don't know. That's why I put the question. You are suggesting that perhaps we know more about Al Capone than juries have been able to conclude over the years. I don't know quite how to go about handling this. Should I call him a crook?

MR. DANIEL: I say, call him a Chicago businessman. Call your friend here an Italian income tax evader. [Laughter.] I don't know what you—call him. But this isn't really material to the matter, because he is going to stay out of jail anyway. I don't know what you are worrying about. [Laughter.] And he's not going to be deported to Italy. You want to bet me five bucks? [Laughter.]

MR. SCHWEID: He's 70 years old. You'll have to give me odds. [Laughter.]

MISS GIRTH: I thought I understood you to say that if the press had really created a situation where a fair trial could not be held you felt it was in the public interest to let the defendant go free rather than put more restrictions on the press.

My question is: At what point in time would that determination be made and who would make it? I would suggest that sometimes when trials are transferred it is not just to protect the judge's reputation; it is to try to give the guy a fair trial somewhere else.

MR. DANIEL: I didn't say those things that you attributed to me. I quoted Mr. John Hart Ely, an Ameri-

can lawyer, writing about the English system and com-
paring it with ours, and I quoted Judge Skelly Wright
of the Circuit Court of Appeals.

I think the answer to your question is that it would
be for the judge to determine. He would determine it at
any point that he concuded that it was just impossible
to get a jury that would give the man a fair trial.

I can't imagine this happening very often. I offered
it as testimony from two distinguished members of the
bar and the bench who seem to feel that maintaining
freedom of the press is more important than letting an
occasional criminal escape now and then.

JOHAN BENSON, House Committee on Government Operations: I have a question which seems to
follow up the question asked by the man from *The
Washington Post*. Would these regulations which are
proposed and adopted here really answer the question
that you were speaking to? I think that they are actually
constraints upon lawyers and not upon members of the
press as to when they can release information.

It says here, reading over Justice Reardon's statement,
that "while prior criminal records of the accused would
not be officially released by prosecutors or law enforcement agencies, the news media could, if they choose to,
publish what their own files contain."

I suppose that these regulations refer to the lawyers
and law enforcement officials. There is another area that
you have been addressing some of your remarks to which
is what judges would do if the press did publish other

things which were not constrained by these regulations. That may be another area of consideration.

MR. DANIEL: If you go to the final section of the Reardon Report relating to contempt actions against those who willfully make statements designed to influence the outcome of the trial, you will find the sentence to which I am referring.

It might be that we are ultimately going to have to have the Supreme Court decide whether my interpretation of this is right or not. I hope we do. I think we should.

I think if this Reardon Report is ever put into practice, which I sometimes doubt, that cases of this sort will go to the Supreme Court. The Supreme Court will have to decide whether it is proper for judges to put newspapermen in jail for contempt of court for publishing things that judges tell them not to publish. We shall see.

I happen to believe that it is unconstitutional but I am certainly not a lawyer and I don't purport to know what the law is. We have a lawyer here who maybe will tell us.

PROFESSOR WILLSON: Mr. Daniel, I want to assure you that I hold *The New York Times* in at least as high regard as the American Bar Association, *The Washington Post,* and the *Louisville Courier-Journal,* as well. But I wish I shared your optimism about Keokuk. I wonder if you think that it's really fair to cite as a statistic a fraction of 1 percent of felonies reported in

the *New York Daily News* when the vast majority of
American daily papers have circulations under 25,000,
and they report every felony and quite a number of
misdemeanors?

Your trickle-down philosophy about the good intentions of the major newspapers in the country, do you
think that this will achieve something in perhaps the
same amount of time as imposition of Judge Reardon's
recommendations?

MR. DANIEL: I think you have a reasonable point
to which the press should address itself. First of all, I
chose the *Daily News* for the simple reason that it is in
most people's mind the epitome of the tabloid newspaper, which is or seems to be a sensational newspaper.
The *Daily News* is not nearly as sensational as people like
to imagine that it is, but it does deal more in crime than
the average big-city newspaper, certainly far more than
any newspaper in New York. I chose it deliberately for
that reason.

But of course you are right. In a small town a felony
is probably bigger news in that constituency than it is in
New York. That is perfectly true. But perhaps instead
of speculating about how they handle news in Keokuk,
and I chose that name out of the air simply because it's
a funny name, perhaps we ought to look at some newspapers in Keokuk.

I cited you the example of the handling of the Mossler
case. Those 30 newspapers were not all big city newspapers.

PROFESSOR WILLSON: How about Miami? Was that in the study?

MR. DANIEL: Miami gave a great deal of attention to that case. It was a local news story and of great interest in that community. I am perfectly aware of it. But how much space did the *Miami Herald* actually give to it, do you know? [No response.] No, you don't, you see. You just think you know or you just imagine that you know. Now, it would be instructive—

MR. WILLSON: I just imagine that the statistics on 30 other newspapers around the country are rather meaningless.

MR. DANIEL: It would be instructive for you, but I also ask you to recall, if you will, what happened to Mrs. Mossler and her nephew? What happened to them?

VOICES: They were acquitted.

MR. DANIEL: They were acquitted. They were acquitted. They didn't get a fair trial, these poor people. The *Miami Herald* so prejudiced the jury down there that these people couldn't get a fair trial. Isn't it terrible? It's just awful.

The *Miami Herald*, I am sure, gave that trial full coverage during the trial. But how many columns of news does the *Miami Herald* print a day? I don't know. A very small proportion of it was given to the Mossler trial and those people who were interested in it I'm sure ate it up. It was printed in great quantity in the *Daily News* in New York and I ate it up. That's the only place

I could get it. I couldn't get it in *The New York Times.*
[Laughter.]

MR. PIERSON: You have suggested that Part IV of
the Reardon Report might be declared unconstitutional.
I agree with you; I think that would be the result. Then
what have you to say about the other parts? Would you
quite agree with those?

MR. DANIEL: Perhaps I wasn't explicit enough but
I repeat what I said near the end of my remarks: That
I have no objection to any restraints that the bar, the
police, or the judiciary may wish to place upon themselves. Does that answer your question?

MR. PIERSON: Yes, sir. As I understand it then, if
Part IV is declared unconstitutional, you are quite happy
with the rest of the Reardon Report?

MR. DANIEL: I am perfectly happy with the
Reardon Report, provided, as I said, these separate professions mind their own business and don't interfere with
the press.

MR. PIERSON: To clarify it still further, Part I
makes some modification of Canon 20, in an attempt to
make more detailed the canon which has not been enforced up to date. Part III concerns the judiciary; it
does involve the press in the closed hearings. Part II
concerns law-enforcement agencies. The Reardon Report proposes that, unless the law enforcement agencies
themselves adopt something like these provisions, the
judiciary impose them. Do you favor that?

MR. DANIEL: No, sir. I repeat: As long as they

wish to discipline themselves. I don't think it's up to the lawyers to try to run the executive branch of the government. I don't think it's up to the lawyers to determine what should be printed in the newspapers. And I don't think that judges ought to be putting newspapermen in jail for doing what I think is their duty. But, if lawyers wish to exercise some restraint in their own profession, if police wish to exercise restraint in their business, and if judges wish to exercise their prerogatives, not only restraint on themselves but the prerogatives they already have—and they are quite considerable—I have no objection. Justice Clark, as I told you, seems to think the judges have powers enough.

These powers are being exercised right now, you know, Mr. Pierson. In this very week in New York, there has been a closed hearing in the case of a woman accused of murdering her child. (Incidentally, that's another one of these cases that is four years old.)

In any case, you haven't heard any newspapers in New York shouting and screaming about this. You've seen no editorials about it. You've seen nobody trying to break into the courtroom. You've seen nobody trying to steal the records of the case.

This is perfectly legitimate. We understand the reason for it. The question before the judge at a pre-trial hearing is whether certain statements this woman made to the police some time ago should be admissible at the trial. Nobody is objecting.

But, to carry on beyond this, to encourage the judges

in a highly restrictive policy—you only have to give them an inch and they'll take ten yards, you know—is in my view wrong and dangerous and damaging to freedom of the press.

MR. PIERSON: I am merely asking a clarifying question because most of what you have said I find I am in complete agreement with, so I am not being argumentative about it. I do think one thing should be said about ABA, because it gets very little defense here. On the speedy trial question the ABA does have committees that have spent an enormous amount of time trying to develop new means of speeding up jurisprudence, particularly criminal jurisprudence. This wasn't really within the jurisdiction of Judge Reardon's committee, but there was a committee of which his group was a subcommittee, which has trial speed-ups within its broad jurisdiction. So I don't think you can attribute to him a lack of interest in it.

But I quite agree with you that judges ought not to substitute their judgment for the executive.

Do you believe that state legislatures would impose the Reardon requirements upon the executive?

MR. DANIEL: So far as it is within the province of the state legislatures and it isn't in conflict with the state constitutions or the federal Constitution, certainly. The legislature, as far as I am concerned, is supreme in these matters. It can make whatever rules it likes.

I am not opposed at all to the new reticence being shown by the police so long as the press is left entirely free to expose a good deal of the chicanery that goes on, as you very well know, behind the closed doors of the police station. We don't want the doors of the police stations of this country closed in the faces of the public. The only representative the public has there, besides the lawyers who go to the defense of people who are arrested, is the press.

MR. PIERSON: Do you think that the judiciary is proper in handling its own affairs through closed hearings?

MR. DANIEL: I think closed hearings are in order in some cases, as I have just said.

MR. PIERSON: Thank you.

MR. FREEBURG: I don't have a question. I was going to make an observation and speak to Keokuk, which Mr. Willson brought up. I was reared in Galesburg, Illinois, which is not too far from Keokuk. Galesburg was a town of 30,000. We had one afternoon newspaper and there wasn't anything that took place in that town that everyone didn't know before the paper ever came out. I'm sure this was the same in Keokuk.

So I don't see where anything could be printed in a paper in a town of that size which wouldn't be known. Much more than was actually in the paper would be known by the people in the town just by word of mouth.

MR. DANIEL: I think Mr. Freeburg makes a good point. You know, local newspapers quite often—and I've worked on them and lived in small towns—are often far more reticent than the women of the town.

[Laughter.] It bears again on my point that pre-trial publicity isn't only printed but it is said by word of mouth.

MR. FREEBURG: The question in many of these towns most of the time is: Why didn't they print this?

MR. BENSON: Isn't it a problem once you get it out, when it gets to the written word and the printed page, that it acquires a new kind of authority and force?

MR. DANIEL: I'm glad you have this confidence in newspapers. I don't.

MR. BENSON: It's not only confidence but a lack of confidence in the people who interpret them.

RUSSELL EAGAN: Mr. Daniel, I happen to be a lawyer and my question doesn't necessarily reflect my viewpoint, but I wonder this. I understand you to have said in effect that you have no quarrel with the bar's in effect dealing with people subject to its jurisdiction, that is with the professions and the police officers. I wonder if there might still not be a problem area. For example, the question was asked at this session last week: Suppose that you have in your files information concerning a prior record and you determine that the facts justify that you print this, but you are not satisfied as to whether your files are entirely accurate. Would you be disturbed if the effect of this Reardon Report were that you would have no source to check what should be public records to bring your file up to date?

MR. DANIEL: Yes, I am disturbed with the closing of public records. The question I don't think has been put quite that way this evening. I think public records should be public records, that's all.

MR. EAGAN: I am thinking of the sealing of the list on prior records, and I am not clear as to the full import of that. I understand the prosecutor isn't supposed to make it available. I am not clear as to whether the press can go in and search the public records.

MR. DANIEL: I'm not clear either. I don't know, but I think I know what the intent of the Reardon Report is. It is that those things would not be made available by public officials, which I think is—

MR. EAGAN: This wouldn't bar you from inspecting public records.

MR. DANIEL: I sincerely hope not but I don't happen to know.

MR. EAGAN: If the Reardon Report were to bar you, would that bother you?

MR. DANIEL: It certainly would. I obviously rather like the view expressed by Mr. Katzenbach, which was that public records are public records, and if a newspaperman comes around and asks for them he can have them.

THIRD SESSION

(Editor's Note: The confrontation of Justice Reardon and *New York Times* managing editor Daniel, in the third session of this Rational Debate, took place in the National Press Club on May 16, 1968. It became the first in a series of National Press Club Town Meetings; it was televised by the Metromedia network on its program, "Face to Face," and was broadcast by radio and television stations in several cities, including Washington, New York, Pittsburgh, Boston, and San Francisco. The transcript has been slightly edited for clarity, with the approval of the principals.)

WARREN ROGERS, Washington Bureau Chief, *Look* Magazine and Moderator of the Metromedia program, "Face to Face": Good evening, I'm Warren Rogers, substituting for Mark Evans who is the regular host on this program. The name of the program is "Face to Face." The issue is Free Press versus Fair Trial, originating from Washington's famous National Press Club and presented with the cooperation of the American Enterprise Institute, which is a nonpartisan educational organization. We have on our platform two of the most distinguished advocates of the principles guaranteed in our First and Sixth Amendments, the freedom of the press and the right of every person accused of a crime to a fair trial by jury. Though these gentlemen are in agreement on these basic rights, they are in complete—almost complete—disagreement on the accommodation between the two.

Each of our guests has argued his case in a Rational Debate Seminar sponsored by the American Enterprise Institute. Tonight they meet for the first time Face to Face.

Let me introduce them. Judge Paul Reardon became Chief Justice of the Superior Court of Massachusetts in 1955 and was elevated to Associate Justice of the Supreme Court of Massachusetts in 1962. He was chairman of the Advisory Committee on Fair Trial and Free Press of the American Bar Association, whose recommendations, adopted by the House of Delegates of the ABA, started a nationwide controversy. Judge Reardon, you are welcome to "Face to Face." [Applause.]

Clifton Daniel, after a distinguished career as a reporter on the national and international scenes, is now manager editor of *The New York Times*. He opposes much of the Reardon Report and considers it a threat to the traditional freedom of the press. Mr. Daniel, welcome to "Face to Face." [Applause.]

The ground rules for "Face to Face" are simple. They are based on fairness and equal time. First Mr. Daniel will present a brief summary of his stand on Free Press and Fair Trial. Judge Reardon will then state his position. Each man will be given time to answer the arguments of his opponent. I shall be the arbiter, and, in this case, Judge Reardon, I shall be the judge of fairness.

After a reasonable time to state their respective positions and to bring the issues into focus, the program will be opened to questions from the audience. Our audience is composed of representatives of the press, the legal profession, the judiciary, the academic world, and other concerned citizens who are gathered here at the National Press Club. Let's start with Mr. Daniel.

MR. DANIEL: Mr. Rogers, I think I can state my position, or the position of the American press, very briefly in this matter. (Mr. Daniel read the last section of his rebuttal text.)

MODERATOR ROGERS: Thank you, Mr. Daniel. Judge Reardon, will you summarize the position of the American Bar Association?

JUSTICE REARDON: Mr. Moderator, ladies and gentlemen. As nearly everyone is aware, the First Amendment of the Bill of Rights of the United States Constitution provides that Congress shall make no law abridging the freedom of speech or of the press. The Sixth Amendment provides that defendants in criminal prosecution shall enjoy the right to a speedy and public trial by an impartial jury of the state and district wherein the crime shall have been committed.

For a great many years thinking citizens have been

troubled by a supposed incompatibility between these two Amendments and by the impact of prejudicial publicity on the administration of criminal justice. In the last three and a half years I have been chairman of a national committee which has sought methods of preserving and strengthening the right to a fair trial without abridging freedom of speech and of the press.

Our committee, which in its membership contained men with years of experience in prosecuting, defending, and judging cases, came to conclude that the primary burden for insuring a fair trial rested on the legal branch and the agencies which serve and minister to it. We concluded also that there was an accommodation possible which would give full force to the guarantees of the First and Sixth Amendments without simultaneously giving rise to conflicts which have in many quarters been deemed inevitable.

With that belief, we recommended an adoption of limitations, carefully defined as to content and timing, on the release of information bearing on the apprehension and trial of defendants by members of the bar and by law enforcement agencies, with appropriate remedies available where there had been a showing that a fair trial had been jeopardized.

What we are talking about this evening largely concerns the reaction of the American news media to these recommendations of ours, which were principally designed to clean up our own house, by which I mean the bench, the bar, and the enforcement agencies.

I hope that the discussion of the next hour may throw some light on the subject of Fair Trial—Free Press and aid you in an understanding of our proposals, what they are, what they are not, and of the debate which has attended since they were announced in October, 1966.

MODERATOR ROGERS: Thank you, Judge Reardon.

Mr. Daniel, do you have anything to say about that statement of the Judge's?

MR. DANIEL: Well, Mr. Rogers, Justice Reardon says that the purpose of his committee was to carry out the mandate of the Sixth Amendment of the Constitution, which provides for a speedy and public trial by an impartial jury. The committee seemed to take the attitude that the one single thing in all this world that might influence the impartiality of a jury unfavorably was publicity in newspapers or on the radio or on television.

When offered the opportunity to await the results of a study to determine whether this was indeed a fact, whether juries were indeed influenced by publicity in the press, Justice Reardon's committee declined the opportunity. Very early it decided against making such an investigation itself. Although the committee, as Justice Reardon has said, made six massive studies of this question, not one of those studies went to the very basic question in this matter, and that is whether pre-trial publicity—which is what the committee so much concerns itself with—actually influences juries in any material way.

With all respect to Justice Reardon, other jurists of equal distinction who have studied this matter have decided against any number of recommendations made by Justice Reardon's committee. I can mention a few of them—whom Justice Reardon knows very well— Judge Medina of the Circuit Court of Appeals, Judge Kaufman of the Circuit Court of Appeals, former Associate Justice of the Supreme Court Tom Clark. Justice Clark, I believe, has stated that he found that the rules proposed by the Reardon committee were unnecessary, that the judges in this country already had sufficient powers to deal with the problems raised by the Reardon committee.

MODERATOR ROGERS: Mr. Daniel, you have raised a number of objections and criticisms here. Before you go on, I think we would like to have something from the Judge here as to what you have already said.

JUSTICE REARDON: Our studies indicated that there had been interference with trials by the prejudice of juries. One such case was *Juelich* v. *The United States,* which is a recent case: After considerable pre-trial news coverage referring to the defendants as murderers and reporting their prior record, every member of the jury ultimately impaneled admitted having an opinion as to guilt.

In the case of the *United States ex rel Bloeth* v. *Denno,* of 38 prospective jurors questioned, 36 stated they had read about the case and 31 stated they had formed an opinion as to guilt. Of the 16 jurors selected, including four alternates, only one denied knowledge of the case, and eight admitted to an opinion.

The empirical jury study which has been suggested is a highly desirable thing. But we felt that we had enough information to warrant our conclusion that there was an interference with a fair jury trial by some of the publicity which was getting through to the jurors. We said in our report that we were in favor of empirical jury studies. We favor them but we saw no reason to hold up the recommendations of the report pending those studies.

As a matter of fact, the problem of prejudicial publicity involves not only its effect upon the jurors, but it involves the integrity of the whole criminal process itself. The administration of criminal justice should not be in a carnival atmosphere. And if there were no effect of prejudicial publicity of any kind upon the jurors at all, nonetheless it should be that justice is seen to be done.

For these reasons we felt no need to hold up pending the empirical jury studies which were projected by the editors and the publishers.

MODERATOR ROGERS: Do you buy that, Mr. Daniel?

MR. DANIEL: It seems to me that Justice Reardon is making an extraordinary point for a judge. He is saying that he feels it's perfectly all right to go ahead and render the verdict before receiving all the evidence.

He says that it would be highly desirable to have empirical studies óf jury behavior but his committee felt it had enough information without making such a study.

I respectfully contend that those gentlemen didn't have enough information. The Judge has cited two or three or four cases. Let me cite two that are perhaps well known to this audience, made up mainly of laymen. Let me cite the trial of Dr. Coppolino, who was accused in New Jersey of murdering his best friend. The trial was held in Freehold, New Jersey. The most prejudicial kind of publicity about Dr. Coppolino was published in the newspapers all over the country, and some of it was published, I might add, in *The New York Times*. It was said that it was impossible for Dr. Coppolino to get a fair trial in the circumstances. In particular, one item published in *The New York Times* was an article warmly praising the principal prosecution witness, Dr. Helpern, the New York medical examiner, saying that he was virtually infallible.

As a matter of fact, the jury in Freehold, New Jersey, didn't believe Dr. Helpern and released Dr. Coppolino. He subsequently was convicted in Florida on another charge and by another jury and on other evidence.

Perhaps the most notorious trial we have had since the Sheppard trial, about which so much has been said, perhaps the most notorious one we have had in many years aside from the Coppolino trial, was the Mossler trial in Miami, Florida. There it was alleged that the newspapers gave extraordinary publicity to the proceedings. The trial was surrounded by a "carnival atmosphere," to use Justice Reardon's phrase. It is true that enormous publicity was given to this in the papers in Miami where the trial was heard. In actual fact not very much publicity was given to it outside Miami. But there in the jurisdiction where the trial was conducted, enormous publicity was given to it.

And what was the result? Mrs. Mossler, who was accused in collaboration with her nephew of murdering her husband, was in fact acquitted.

How can one say that the jury in such a case was prejudiced?

MODERATOR ROGERS: Justice Reardon, there is a question for you.

JUSTICE REARDON: Well, possibly in that case one cannot say the jury was prejudiced. But you have selected two cases which you have spoken of to a considerable extent in speeches here and elsewhere.

But I would like to ask you a question, Mr. Daniel. Exactly what is it in our report with which you quarrel?

MR. DANIEL: The matter is very simple, Justice Reardon. I think you know, but perhaps the audience doesn't. I quarrel very seriously with any processes or any procedures or any proposals that will make trials in this country more secret. That's number one. Number two—

MODERATOR ROGERS: Let's get the reaction to number one.

MR. DANIEL: Very well.

JUSTICE REARDON: All right now. Your own *Times* in an editorial on the Dioguerdi case back eight or nine years ago stated: "The press cannot be expected to refrain from printing statements issued by public officials, as for example, the United States Attorney, even though such statements may be prejudicial to a fair trial. The only way to stop this abuse is to stop it at the source."

MR. DANIEL: Right.

JUSTICE REARDON: That is what we have tried to do. Just to continue along a little bit, when our recommendations came out last October your *Times* stated: "The ABA Report recognizes that many, if not most, of the current infractions by the press of the right of fair trial stem from extrajudicial comments from law enforcement officials and attorneys. It lays down strict regulations enforceable through such penalties as disbarment and contempt citations to restrict the release of information that might prejudice a juror. We have long held that this is the most effective method of tackling the problem."

MR. DANIEL: Excuse me, sir, but you haven't—

JUSTICE REARDON: Do you agree with that?

MR. DANIEL: I agree with every word of that.

But you haven't addressed yourself to the point I made, which was that the Reardon Report adopted by the House of Delegates of the American Bar Association very seriously encourages the holding of secret hearings.

You haven't mentioned that at all, sir. Let's hear what you have to say about that.

JUSTICE REARDON: Well, the answer to that is that what you have just said simply is not so. What the report states is that when there is a question of evidence and a question of admissibility of evidence which, if it were laid before the jury in public, might prejudice the trial, the hearing will be held in camera but that a transcript of that hearing will be kept and that the public in due course will be advised of everything that transpired.

MR. DANIEL: In due course what? Nine years later, ten years later?

JUSTICE REARDON: Now, you made that statement in the speech which you made here last week—

MR. DANIEL: Yes, sir.

JUSTICE REARDON:—and that's a perfectly ridiculous statement, and I'll tell you why. If you will read our report you will see that we are not holding up the release of information until the case has gone through the appellate court. We are holding—

MR. DANIEL: I'm not saying what—

JUSTICE REARDON:—that information—

MR. DANIEL:—you do, sir. I am saying what your report proposes.

JUSTICE REARDON: The report proposes the withholding of that information until the conclusion of the trial and the sentence of the defendant. And that is not any eight or nine years in the vast majority of cases.

MR. DANIEL: At the current time, at this moment, there is a case—it's a very simple case really—a hijacking case being tried in New York, that has been pending for nine years. If there had been a pre-trial hearing held in that case nine years ago, we would not until this day be allowed to publish that in the newspapers in New York according to the rules and regulations prescribed by the Reardon Report.

JUSTICE REARDON: It seems that the *Times* might well address itself to the problem of delay in that particular case.

MR. DANIEL: That's what I want the Reardon committee, the ABA, and the legal profession to address themselves to.

MODERATOR ROGERS: We come now to the special feature of "Face to Face," questions from the audience. Will you please state your name, your affiliation and be as brief as possible, please, in the interest of time. Address your question either to Mr. Daniel or to Judge Reardon. One question per person, please, so that as many of you as possible may be heard. Now the first question.

WALTER GARVER, United States Chamber of Commerce: I am neither a journalist nor a lawyer, and I am here as one of your concerned citizens.

It seems to me as a citizen that there is increasing doubt about the integrity and the relevance of our judicial system. In the first place, more and more of the decisions are based on technicalities and complexities within the law. This has seemed to many of us to make it a sort of occult or mystic lodge which we can't comprehend. Secondly, while all are equal before the bar of justice, it seems that some are more equal than others. It is common talk in the street that one's success in court depends on his financial resources either in employing skilled counsel or going beyond to the ultimate course of appeal, and so forth.

So my question, then, to Justice Reardon is this: With this doubt and these uncertainties, isn't it a grave risk we are taking of the probability of further destroying confidence in the judicial system and processes if we draw further restrictions or further veils of secrecy, further alienating the citizen from the judicial and court processes?

JUSTICE REARDON: Well, Mr. Garver, first of all, you have made a number of assumptions with which I am in complete and thorough disagreement. When a penniless Clarence Gideon down in Florida seeks counsel, he gets the best counsel in the United States. And there are plenty instances of that. And it does not seem to me that while we are discussing the subject of Fair Trial-Free Press tonight I have to launch into a defense of the American judicial system.

The second assumption you have made, as did indeed Mr. Daniel, is that we are fostering secret trials. I deny it. I say that the only time when hearings are closed is when there will be evidence which may or may not be inadmissible which would prejudice the fair outcome of that trial. That evidence will subsequently be divulged. The only punishments or sanctions that are at all recommended in our recommendations have to do with contempt proceedings in the most grievous of cases.

I think the American press has failed to read the contempt provisions of this report, which in effect narrowly limit the imposition of contempt and are much less than the inherent powers of the courts as they now exist. That is the way I would answer your question.

LUTHER HUSTON, *Editor and Publisher*: I may be asking a question of both Justice Reardon and Mr. Daniel. Since the assassination of Dr. Martin Luther King the Justice Department and the FBI have given out a lot of background information about the alleged assassin, James Earl Ray or whatever his name is. Now I realize that giving that out and having that published in the paper may aid the law enforcement agencies in their attempts to capture this man. But isn't it also true that, as was said after the assassination of President Kennedy, that Lee Harvey Oswald, after all the publicity there, could not have gotten a fair trial before any jury in the United States?

Now I wonder, when Mr. Ray or whatever his name is is captured, could he get a fair trial?

MODERATOR ROGERS: You address that to Judge Reardon or to Mr. Daniel?

MR. HUSTON: Judge Reardon.

JUSTICE REARDON: One of the reasons which gave rise to the foundation of our committee was the

Warren Commission Report upon the shambles in Dallas. It was generally agreed that Lee Harvey Oswald could not have received a fair trial anywhere in these United States. Now, while there are those who contend that that's all right and that there are notorious cases which the democracy demands be out in the open to the extent that there can never be a fair trial, we disagree with that. We say the most miserable wretch in our society is entitled to a fair trial and that applies to assassins no matter who they may be. That's about all that I would say, Mr. Rogers.

MODERATOR ROGERS: Mr. Daniel, do you have any comment on that question?

MR. DANIEL: First of all, the Warren Commission and Justice Reardon at this moment have said that Lee Harvey Oswald could not have had a fair trial in Texas or anywhere in these United States, given the circumstances of his arrest and exposure to the press. Yet, as Justice Reardon knows, the Warren Commission then turned around and gave Lee Harvey Oswald a trial in which it found him guilty. It found that he had not conspired with others, that he had acted alone. It found out an enormous amount about him which it then certified to the public as being the truth or the facts.

I happen to agree with the Warren Commission, but to say that the Warren Commission, which happened to be made up of distinguished citizens, jurists, and others, could give Lee Harvey Oswald a fair trial and then turn around and say that 12 good men and true, chosen to serve on a jury in Dallas, couldn't have done the same thing seems to me to be quite inconsistent.

I feel that Oswald could have had a fair trial. A fair trial doesn't always necessarily mean acquittal, you know. Fair trial sometimes means conviction and when all the evidence was in the jury might very well have convicted Lee Harvey Oswald. But I see no reason to assume that the trial would have been unfair.

If the Warren Commission can do it, a jury of good sound citizens could do the same thing.

MR. HUSTON: Judge Reardon, you said every wretch is entitled to a fair trial.

JUSTICE REARDON: I think I said miserable wretch.

MR. HUSTON: Yes, miserable wretch. The word that intrigues me is "entitled." Do you think, even though entitled, that every miserable wretch does indeed get a fair trial?

JUSTICE REARDON: I said he is entitled to a fair trial.

MR. HUSTON: Entitled to it.

JUSTICE REARDON: One of the reasons that he doesn't get a fair trial is the area in which we have been working so that he can get one.

MODERATOR ROGERS: The next question.

JUSTICE REARDON: I'd like to make one more comment before I forget it. The publishers and editors have been meeting together lately. In reading of their goings on relative to our report I can only think of that deathless line from Robert Service: A bunch of the boys were whooping it up in the Malamute Saloon—[laughter]—because when Editor Murray of the *Arizona Republic* asked the editors here in Washington at the Shoreham Hotel, which is the local Malamute Saloon of the time—[laughter]—how many of them had read the report, by his estimate only 25 percent of the editors had read it. He quipped later that he had given them a long count. [Laughter.]

I'd like to toss in a statistic of my own on that. I'll wager, if it's legal in the District of Columbia, that of that 75 percent who haven't read it 80 percent have editorialized upon it and given us the usual massive assault.

MR. DANIEL: May I put in a word here? [Laughter.]

MODERATOR ROGERS: You may.

MR. DANIEL: First of all, I can assure Justice Reardon that those editors that I know about, including Ed Murray, have read the report and they have read it most carefully and studied it most diligently. Those who have written editorials on it, I believe, have all read it.

I'd like to ask a question also. How many members of the American Bar Association have read it?

JUSTICE REARDON: I wouldn't know.

MR. DANIEL: I'll make you the same wager about the bar that you make about the press.

JUSTICE REARDON: I would doubt that very much. There were—

MR. DANIEL: You doubt it, sir, but I'll be glad to take a poll. [Laughter.]

JUSTICE REARDON: I tell you, at Chicago, when we voted that in, there were—

MR. DANIEL: How many were in Chicago? 275.

JUSTICE REARDON: I'll tell you who were at Chicago in addition to delegates. There were members of the press whom we invited to state their case. But when the editors met here in Washington there were no lawyers on the panel. This is Mr. Mollenhoff's word: Chairman Murray declared this was a "conscious decision," based on the theory that there was no need to confuse the issue and to provide a further sounding board for the legal profession. [Laughter.] Now they consider that a fair trial. [Applause.]

MR. DANIEL: It sounds to me, sir, rather like your statement: You don't want to hear any more evidence— "We already know the facts"—and I cite that quotation.

JUSTICE REARDON: I have read a thousand editorials on this subject and—

MR. DANIEL: Not editorials, sir, the facts.

JUSTICE REARDON: There is a difference?

MR. DANIEL: Yes, sir. [Laughter.]

JUSTICE REARDON: I admit it, and you've said— [laughter and applause].

MODERATOR ROGERS: Somebody mentioned Mr. Mollenhoff and I see he's standing up here patiently waiting to ask a question.

CLARK MOLLENHOFF, *Des Moines Register:* First let me say that—

JUSTICE REARDON: Just a minute. Before you say a word, Mr. Mollenhoff. You were out at another keening and wailing conference in Minneapolis with that Sigma Delta Chi.

MR. MOLLENHOFF: That's correct. [Laughter.]

JUSTICE REARDON: And I ask you whether you were quoted correctly in saying that Judge Reardon, on this report, is a nice gentleman but he's divorced from reality? Did you say that?

MR. MOLLENHOFF: Something like that, a naive something. [Laughter.]

JUSTICE REARDON: Now, let me just say before you ask your question. I accept the first part of that statement with thanks. As to the second part, I harbor the quaint provincial notion, having lived here for several years, that the farther one gets away from Washington the closer one approaches reality. [Laughter and applause.]

Now I'd be glad to have your question, Mr. Mollenhoff.

MR. MOLLENHOFF: I'm not going to argue with you on that particular point. I will say also that I think the press needed the jar, not necessarily of a Reardon Report, but of some proposal in this area. However, I am opposed to the Reardon Report and if the saying that power corrupts and absolute power corrupts absolutely has any substance at all—

JUSTICE REARDON: Lord Acton.

MR. MOLLENHOFF:—then I think that this brings the court into an area of absolute power. I wonder if you have taken into account that under the present court procedures you can do all of the things that you say you need for an antiseptic court operation. If you increase the power in some areas where criminal cases are involved, or where there is fraud in the case of local officials, where the local judiciary has control or it has control with the local sheriff's office, then you are putting too much power into the court's hands, you are tempting the court too much to be dictatorial, to blot out the press from any kind of a reasonable type of an operation.

Let me say that in addition to those corrupt situations which we may find in some cities the same thing would apply if we would get into civil rights cases in the south where you would have a local judge, or a local sheriff who would be tempted and even be given the blessing of the American Bar Association in pulling down a very sharp secrecy. I think this unbalances the situation and I don't think it's needed.

JUSTICE REARDON: Well, I—

A VOICE: Would you repeat the question?

MODERATOR ROGERS: You know, what's so delightful about this program is that everybody ignores the request to be brief. Would you state your point?

MR. MOLLENHOFF: I don't know how to be brief, on this subject. [Laughter.] I merely wanted to find out, if you put your trust, in this area, with these local dictators on the bench who could take this—

JUSTICE REARDON: Alfred Friendly brought that up in an article which he wrote in the *Bulletin of the American Society of Newspaper Editors* just as our studies were announced. I think the best answer for that was to be found in an article in *The Atlantic* last summer by Robert Cipes. He said that if the sheriffs or if the judges who were looking for secrecy in their operations did not have this report at hand they would be using some other excuse. Our report provides no excuse for secrecy and in fact condemns it. This the press, it seems to me, has totally failed to realize: There is no inhibition on the press to expose all the types of corruption which I think you have in mind when you ask that question.

MR. MOLLENHOFF: The Judge Paschen decision, ruling initially in the Speck case out in Illinois, was one that was based upon what you people are studying, your Reardon Report, plus some misinterpretations of the Sheppard case. I think that what you do in this area is to tempt local judiciaries to put too much—

JUSTICE REARDON: On the Paschen case in Peoria, the Speck case was a notorious case, posing a terrific problem for a trial judge. He made his order and the *Tribune* took him into court and two of the segments of the order which he made were removed by the Supreme Court.

What was left of the order was no more than we would have recommended. It correlated very closely with the order which Judge Talty gave in Cleveland in the second Sheppard case. The Paschen order which eventually was left was very close to what we would have recommended as the reasonable operation of a courtroom. When that trial was over, as I recall, Judge Paschen was congratulated by certain members of the press for the manner in which he had handled that case.

MR. MOLLENHOFF: But he had done a service—

MODERATOR ROGERS: Mr. Mollenhoff, I'm afraid that we have run out of time again.

QUESTIONER: My name is Paul Beech and I'm an interested American citizen. My question is directed to Mr. Daniel's opening remarks. Do you really believe that your tongue-in-cheek, levity-laden attitude toward this vital question of fair trial-free press is even a minimally satisfactory position for a representative of the press to take? And do you also believe that freedom of the press is just a constitutional prerogative or is it also a responsibility?

MR. DANIEL: First of all, when you came forward I heard Justice Reardon say, "There's one of my claque."

JUSTICE REARDON: Oh, no. No, no.

MR. DANIEL: I do not believe that my attitude, which was amusing, I hope, and facetious, I certainly admit, represents my total position. I was trying to make a point. But I do entirely agree with you—your point is an excellent one—that the press has a responsibility as well as rights in these matters. You are absolutely right.

JUSTICE REARDON: I don't know the gentleman, Mr. Daniel.

MR. DANIEL: Oh, excuse me.

JUSTICE REARDON: But I thought he asked a very good question. [Laughter.]

MODERATOR ROGERS: The next question, please.

QUESTIONER: My name is Louis Gray and I'm a concerned citizen. This is to Judge Reardon. Wasn't the decision on the original Sheppard case conclusive evidence of pre-trial conviction by the newspapers?

JUSTICE REARDON: Well, the Sheppard case itself deals more with the conduct of the trial and, of course, the publicity which preceded the apprehension of the defendant. The bringing of him to trial has been a hotly-debated subject. But no one can read the pre-trial headlines, no matter how well motivated the editor of the paper which principally was responsible for those headlines, no one can read those headlines without feeling that it would have been almost impossible, almost impossible, given normal reactions of average people, to procure a jury that was unprejudiced in that area. And while Sheppard and Maxwell have gone off largely on other grounds, nonetheless that case contains some elements that indicate that what I have said just now is so.

MR. DANIEL: May I ask a question there? How would Judge Reardon explain the fact that in the same community another jury, which also read those same headlines and also was subjected to that same prejudice, if you like, against Dr. Sam Sheppard was able some years later to acquit him of the same crime of which he was convicted some years ago?

JUSTICE REARDON: I'm not convinced that the circumstances were at all similar as you describe them. Thank you.

MRS. MARY M. AUGLIER: I would like to address the question to Mr. Daniel or perhaps to Justice Reardon. I'm neither a member of the press nor of the bar. I'm a concerned citizen. I recall that there was a freedom of information bill passed last year, I believe in July, by the United States Congress. I would like to ask you, Mr. Daniel, if you see any conflict in this bill and Justice Reardon's Report?

MR. DANIEL: I don't really think they address themselves to the same matter. I don't see any particular conflict between them. The freedom of information bill, I believe, was designed to make information about the operations of our government more available to citizens. I am sure that Justice Reardon would join me in applauding that.

JUSTICE REARDON: I would say so. I would agree.

CHIEF JUDGE J. EDWARD LUMBARD, Chairman of the American Bar Association Committee on Minimum Standards for Criminal Justice: Our committee sponsored Judge Reardon's Report, and my question is for Mr. Daniel. As Mr. Daniel knows, the Reardon committee and its members had numerous discussions over a period of three years with representatives of the news media. During that time was not there some discussion, Mr. Daniel, of whether or not the press could enter into voluntary codes in an attempt to solve the problem of prejudicial publicity? And, if so, what was the result in that connection with respect to voluntary codes.

MR. DANIEL: As everyone who is familiar with the American judiciary knows, Judge Lumbard has been a very active figure in this field, has made a great contribution to it, and I expect he probably knows the answer to this question even better than I do. Statistically speaking, I would say that there have been joint press-bar discussions in some 21 or more states. Voluntary press-bar codes on fair trial have been adopted in perhaps nine or ten. I don't have the figures in front of me. And they are under consideration in six or eight or more states.

I might say at this point that I myself feel that that is the proper solution to this problem: Discussion, debate, agreement, and not an attempt by the bar to set itself up as the judge or the censor or the dominant party in this press-bar disagreement.

Those codes I feel have been effective wherever they have been put into effect. Let's take the case of Oregon. I believe they provided a code and they also provided a means of appeal to anyone who felt the code had been violated. I don't believe that in the four or five years that that code has been in effect anyone has objected that the code was seriously violated.

That, in my view, is the way this matter should be

handled, not through an attempt by the bar to impose its will upon the free press.

JUSTICE REARDON: Mr. Chairman, I can't let that statement go. He's made that statement twice about the bar endeavoring to impose its will on the press and that is far from being the case, very far from being the case. The press is free to print anything that it wishes to print, anything.

MR. DANIEL: No, sir, not according to the contempt powers that you propose the judges should exercise against the press in Part IV of your Report.

JUSTICE REARDON: The contempt powers are not exercisable against the press save in two instances: One —Where there is a willful design to affect an ongoing jury trial. Now, if one were to follow you to the logical conclusion, the American courts would be left defenseless on the face of the most grievous breaches of—

MR. DANIEL: Do you consider the American courts defenseless today, sir?

JUSTICE REARDON: I do not consider them defenseless.

MR. DANIEL: I don't either. And many judges feel that they have sufficient power to deal with this matter, that they don't require any further power.

JUSTICE REARDON: Then you are admitting that those courts must have, right now, the power of contempt.

MR. DANIEL: They have a considerable power. If they don't have—

JUSTICE REARDON: Then we're not arguing about anything.

MR. DANIEL: Well, sir—[laughter]—what I'm arguing about—we'll go back to Mr. Mollenhoff's question —is your committee's lending encouragement to a number of things which are, in our opinion, very dangerous to the freedom of the press in America and to democracy in this country.

First of all, encouragement to the police to keep silent, encouragement to judges to close hearings unnecessarily and indiscriminately and, thirdly, encouragement to judges to threaten the press with contempt proceedings when the press publishes something the judge doesn't happen to like.

JUSTICE REARDON: I hear what you say but I disagree with you. That's all I can say about that. And a fair reading of our report would lead, I think, almost any detached observer to disagree with you.

MODERATOR ROGERS: The next question, please.

RUSSELL FREEBURG, The *Chicago Tribune*: Justice Reardon, I'd like to bring up secrecy again. There is a new murder case in Illinois. Now, for the first time, they have barred from the coroner's inquest newsmen and the public. A coroner's inquest, as I understand it, has no lawful status. So don't you believe that already this shows that there is going to be an unwise extension of your guidelines? This, now, is an example that opens the question: Where is it all going to end?

JUSTICE REARDON: I'd have to accept your assumptions to answer your question in the affirmative and, in any event, I would not be disposed to comment on an ongoing case.

MR. FREEBURG: Could you take a hypothetical situation, then, where just any coroner's inquest was held in secret? Would you believe that this violates your guidelines or goes beyond them?

JUSTICE REARDON: You ruined your second question with your first one. I won't answer it. [Laughter.]

MR. DANIEL: May we ask Justice Reardon to take his own statement made earlier this evening? He said that the rules proposed by the Reardon Report would only close hearings in cases where evidence that might be prejudicial was going to be brought out. That's not what the Reardon Report says. It relates to all kinds of pre-trial hearings, as you well know, sir.

JOHN MacKENZIE, *The Washington Post:* I have read your report and I have read it very carefully. I have looked and have not found any distinction between the rights of free press and free speech. I do have a question, but it seems to me that you could substitute the word free speech every time you talked about free press. Can you see any difference between these two rights? I suggest that one difference may be that the press might have greater access, at least, to the sources of public information.

JUSTICE REARDON: No, the reason why we are talking about interferences with fair trial is because we are engaged in our concerns with the provisions of the Sixth Amendment, which have to do with fair trial; and the freedom of the press is of the most particular concern to fair trial.

We would be talking in much more expansive terms, it seems to me, than we needed to were we to go into the field which you suggest.

MR. MacKENZIE: If it weren't for the press at these hearings that would be closed under the Reardon recommendations, if it were not for the press, would the public be allowed to attend those sessions?

JUSTICE REARDON: You have read the recommendations?

MR. MacKENZIE: Yes.

JUSTICE REARDON: I congratulate you on that, and the recommendations say that the public, including the media, shall be excluded.

MR. MacKENZIE: Yes, and your first draft didn't say, "including the media," did it?

JUSTICE REARDON: No, it did not, and that was put in as a result of asseverations and complaints from various lawyers, many, many hundreds of whom had read the report. I refer back to Mr. Daniel's assertions in that regard. They wished that included because of their personal experiences. So we saw no reason not to include it and we included it.

MR. MacKENZIE: So they're co-equal; the press and the public are co-equal. There is no difference between the public's right and the newspaper reporter's right?

JUSTICE REARDON: I don't know what you're working on there, a syllogism of some sort or other. I've gone along with you so far. I think I'll stop right now. [Laughter.]

MR. MacKENZIE: I was just trying to draw the distinction.

MR. DANIEL: I think, Justice Reardon, that Mr. MacKenzie is making the point that the Sixth Amendment calls for public trials as well as fair ones.

JUSTICE REARDON: That's perfectly correct and yet there has never been, over many years, including in your own state of New York, any disposition to regard a public trial as being a trial which was completely public in all its aspects. Bench conferences have been a part of the trial of cases, for instance, since the Year One and, as a matter of fact, it's your own state of New York which allows closure of preliminary hearings. You have a statute that has been in existence for 80 years. It was that fact which prevailed upon us to recommend it, because New York, in its wisdom, had passed the statute and that was followed by many other states. We considered it a good statute and still do.

MR. DANIEL: We don't want to hold up New York as being wiser than other states, particularly not Massachusetts.

JUSTICE REARDON: I think most native New Yorkers would.

MR. DANIEL: I'm not a native New Yorker.

JUSTICE REARDON: I knew that. [Laughter.]

MIKE MASSETIK, Newhouse Newspapers: There has been some discussion here of the relative competence of the press, *The New York Times* versus other papers. I wonder if we could get into a discussion of the relative competence of judges, particularly state judges, those that face election and then, more particularly, those that face re-election. How are they going to deal with the press or the print media or the television media?

JUSTICE REARDON: You have a very large subject and I would certainly be glad to discuss it with you because it's an area to which I have given a lot of time; but we're not talking about that tonight.

MODERATOR ROGERS: Well, I'll tell you what I'd like you to talk about now, Justice Reardon. I'd like you to talk about your summarized point of view. You've got just about a minute to do it.

JUSTICE REARDON: What we have been working on in these recommendations is something which bothered the late Justice Frankfurter who had great sensitivity in these affairs.

He said, "The moral health of the community is strengthened by according even the most miserable and pathetic of criminals those rights which the Constitution has designed for us all."

And again, concurring in Irvin and Dowd he said: "One of the rightful boasts of Western civilization is that the state has the burden of establishing guilt solely on the basis of evidence produced in court and circumstances assuring an accused all the safeguards of a fair procedure. These rudimentary conditions for determining guilt are inevitably wanting if the jury which is to sit in judgment on a fellow human being comes to its task with its mind ineradically poisoned against him. How can fallible men and women reach a disinterested verdict based exclusively on what they heard in court when, before they entered the jury box, their minds were saturated by press and radio for months preceding by matter designed to establish the guilt of the accused?"

What we have done is try to put limitations upon lawyers, upon enforcement officials, while leaving the press to clean up its own mess; and that is a job in itself.

MODERATOR ROGERS: Mr. Daniel.

MR. DANIEL: If Justice Reardon would do just what he says here instead of what he has recommended to the American Bar Association, we'd have no argument at all. He is not leaving the press alone and that's the substance of our argument.

The Reardon Report, adopted by the House of Delagates of the American Bar Association, and ultimately supposed to be adopted by all of the bar associations of this country, attempts to put into effect in this country news management by the bar and the bench. What's called for is not a dictatorship of one over the other. In these days when we see freedom of the press so highly valued in the countries to the east of us I don't know how we can think about restricting it in this country. What is called for is not a dictatorship by the bar and the bench over the press, but collaboration, cooperation, voluntary agreement to preserve both the free press and fair trial.

MODERATOR ROGERS: Thank you, gentlemen. The controversy over free press and fair trial will continue to be heard around the nation in the press, on radio and television, in the legal profession and among men of good will everywhere. They can disagree about the practice but not the theory and the disagreement will go on for months, perhaps years to come.

PAUL C. REARDON is an associate justice of the Supreme Judicial Court for the Commonwealth of Massachu-setts and served as chairman of the Advisory Committee on Fair Trial-Free Press of the American Bar Association Project on Minimum Standards for Criminal Justice. Earlier he served as Chief Justice of the Superior Court for the Commonwealth of Massachusetts, 1955-62. He is a former member of the Board of Overseers, Harvard University and has been active in American Bar Association affairs for many years.

CLIFTON DANIEL is managing editor of *The New York Times*. As a foreign correspondent with *The New York Times* he served in the Middle East, West Germany, Moscow, London and Paris. He covered the Geneva Summit conference of 1955 and the advance of the First Army into Belgium and Germany in 1944-45. He was a reporter and editor for the Associated Press in Washington, Berne, and London from 1937-43. He won the Overseas Press Club Award, Best Reporting Abroad, in 1955.